Transform Your Culture Through Empowerment

Transform Your Culture Through Empowerment

The Salvarcar Story

San L. Allen

Transform Your Culture Through Empowerment:
The Salvarcar Story

Cover design by Cassandra Kronstedt

Interior design by S4Carlisle Publishing Services, Chennai, India

First published in 2026 by
Business Expert Press, LLC
222 East 46th Street, New York, NY 10017
www.businessexpertpress.com

ISBN-13: 978-1-60649-427-1 (paperback)
ISBN-13: 978-1-60649-428-8 (e-book)

Supply and Operations Management Collection

First edition: 2026

10 9 8 7 6 5 4 3 2 1

EU SAFETY REPRESENTATIVE
Mare Nostrum Group B.V.
Doelen 72
4831 GR Breda
The Netherlands
gpsr@mare-nostrum.co.uk

Description

Transform Your Culture Through Empowerment: The Salvarcar Story is written for those seeking **to develop a transformation system that helps organizations reach their full potential.** It teaches employees how to transform their work systems and to organize and **lead their organizations through the transformation process.** Examples, tools, and techniques are shared. The story of the struggling Salvarcar plant serves as a case study, beginning with the hiring of a new executive tasked with either transforming the organization's operations and culture or shuttering the plant and relocating it. **Real-world examples, issues, innovative solutions, and results illustrate how the facility was transformed into one of the best in its class, ultimately saving it.**

Contents

List of Figures

Preface

Throughout my professional career, I've had the privilege of leading global operations and developing improvement programs that enhance quality and performance across companies in various regions as economies have grown more interconnected. My career has spanned multiple eras, encompassing quality circles, statistical process control (SPC), Six Sigma, Just-in-Time (JIT), simulation, operations research, Lean, white-collar productivity, artificial intelligence (AI), and other initiatives focused on transforming companies to reach their full potential.

Through working with various programs, I realized that they all share the same goal. They rely on concepts rooted in the same principles and are similar in nature. Sometimes, organizations get sidetracked by the chosen methodology rather than focusing on the core essentials for successful transformation. Successful transformation programs depend less on a specific methodology and more on understanding and applying a few key components and processes of a transformation system.

The purpose of this book is to identify and clearly explain a transformation system that can succeed in any organization if followed. The explanation covers the following topics: transformation system and governance, training, innovation, process control, employee evaluations, bonus programs, selecting transformation projects, developing organizational habits, changing culture, and other related items. All of this is illustrated through a case study of a manufacturing facility scheduled for shutdown due to inefficiencies and cost overruns. The facility adopted and implemented a transformation system, subsequently improving from being the worst performing to one of the best in its class.

The reader will learn that transforming an organization and its culture is accomplished through a transformation system. I hope you enjoy reading and applying the transformation keys found in this book. The keys are proven to lead to success.

Acknowledgments

I extend special thanks and gratitude to the staff of Business Expert Press, especially Managing Executive Editor Scott Isenberg, Director of Production and Marketing Charlene Kronstedt, Collection Editor for Supply and Operations Management Joy Field, Cassie Kronstedt, and Gajalakshmi Sivakumar at S4Carlisle Publishing Services for their encouragement and expert assistance in bringing this book to fruition. I also thank my wife, Marsha, for her unwavering love and support. Without her inspiration and patience, this book would not have been written. Additionally, I am grateful to all the colleagues I have worked with over the years for the challenges and victories we shared as we traveled, learned, and succeeded together.

CHAPTER 1
Introduction

In January 2003, I was appointed head of Western Hemisphere Manufacturing for industrial glove production. Our facilities were located in Great Britain, the United States, and Mexico. My first assignment was to lead a complete transformation and cultural change at two struggling manufacturing plants in Cd. Juarez, Mexico. The first plant was the Salvarcar facility, a 215,000 sq. ft. building that housed 1,100 employees and produced 2.0 million pairs of knitted industrial gloves per month in all sizes. The second plant, called Bermudez, was a 75,000 sq. ft. facility that employed 450 people and produced two types of products: nitrile chemical-resistant rubber gloves and palm-dipped foamed nitrile gloves, made from knitted glove liners supplied by the Salvarcar plant. Both glove styles were designed for and used in various industries.

When I joined the company, I planned to spend the first several months focusing on transformation efforts at the Salvarcar facility and then expand these activities to include the Bermudez operation. During my first two weeks at work, I interviewed all the staff and familiarized myself with the operational processes. The purpose of this focus became clear after I reviewed key metrics. The reported measurements raised significant concerns and highlighted the urgent need for transformation.

- Scrap Rate: Was 14 percent.
- Customer Service Shipping Performance: Was 47 percent on time to the committed date.
- Efficiency: Labor efficiency was 45 percent.
- Absenteeism: The average daily rate was 1.5 percent.
- Monthly Turnover: Was 8 percent, much higher than the city average of 3.5 percent.
- Average Cycle Time: Was three weeks from job order release to shipment.

- Number of Pay Levels: Was 72 levels for the hourly employees.
- Plant Efficiency: 1,100 employees produced 2.0 million pairs of gloves per month.
- Inventory Cycle Count Accuracy: Was 70 percent.
- Finances: Were significantly negative compared to the standard budget.

In week 3, the president of the global company flew in to meet with me in person and provide direction. After taking a quick tour of the manufacturing facility, we had a guidance session that included the following conversation:

PRESIDENT: 'San, you have been here for a couple of weeks and have had a chance to see the facility and meet the people. What is your plan?'

SAN: 'I plan to learn more about the operations and customer base over the next two months; then, I will start making changes.'

PRESIDENT: 'Hum, that is not a good plan. If this operation is not turned around or shows dramatic improvement over the next 6 months, it will be shut down, and the operation will be moved to Southeast Asia.'

SAN: 'I wish you had mentioned that during the interview process. It seems like an important piece of information that was left out.'

PRESIDENT: 'Yeah, I was afraid you wouldn't accept the opportunity if that were stated. Anyway, that's the plan. We better start making changes this month. We'll talk each month to see how it goes.'

With that, he wished me well and offered his best for great success before he left. Six months isn't much time. What were we supposed to do?

This scenario may sound extreme, but it's a familiar story. This really happened to me! We successfully navigated the first six months as a team and completely transformed the operation over the next three years. The transformation results for the Salvarcar facility were:

- Total operating expenses decreased by 33.3 percent. Non-raw material expenses were reduced by 60 percent.
- Scrap Rate: Reduced to 1.5 percent.

- Customer Service Shipping Performance: Increased to 99.0 percent.
- Efficiency: Increased to 112 percent.
- Absenteeism: Reduced to 0.8 percent.
- Monthly Turnover: Reduced to 0.9 percent.
- Average Cycle Time: Reduced to three hours per order.
- Number of Pay Levels: Reduced to 20.
- Plant Efficiency: 800 employees produce 4.0 million pairs per month.
- Inventory Cycle Count Accuracy: Increased to 99.5 percent.
- Inventories: Reduced by 60 percent.
- Floor Space: 40 percent of the floor space became available.
- A long waiting list for hourly positions formed as people added their names to a will-call list for openings. They would leave their jobs at other companies to take positions at the Salvarcar facilities as they became available.
- The facility established itself as a global best-in-class location.
- Finances: very favorable

The professional staff at Salvarcar participated in all transformation activities. They brought a diverse mix of ages, experiences, tenures, educations, cultures, and other characteristics. Despite their differences, they came to work each day prepared to collaborate, utilizing their skills to help transform the culture and achieve the goals of this major turnaround project. Their impressive achievements demonstrate what can be accomplished through effort, organization, a solid transformation system, and teamwork. The Salvarcar story will be featured throughout the book.

All Things Are the Same

My children, grandchildren, friends, and co-workers have often heard me repeat the phrase, "All things are the same, just the variables change." The older I get and the more experience I gain, the more I believe this phrase. Some may think, "If the variables change, how can all things be the same?" It is accurate to say that not everything is physically or conceptually the same. In many ways, a computer is different from a glass of water, an automatically generated report, or an organization. However, they are largely the same in many respects: each serves a purpose. Each system contains the building blocks of processes that take inputs and generate outputs. Each system can be broken down into one or more sublevel systems, each containing more detailed processes, inputs, and outputs. All systems can be analyzed and modified using standard tools, techniques, and methods. System outputs change only when inputs or processes change.

For example, when viewed from space, Earth appears glorious and is seen as a living biosphere system. That biosphere system is composed of many subsystems, which are then composed of subsystems, and those are composed of lower-level subsystems until we get down to the atom, which is again composed of subsystems. Looking in the other direction, the Earth is a subsystem of our solar system, which is a subsystem of the Milky Way Galaxy, which is a subsystem of the universe.

Each subsystem has a process. Each process can be mapped into segments and measured. It seems that the same can be said for most things on Earth. Human bodies, companies, teams, buildings, governments, cultures, religions, habits, and other entities are created by a process, perform a process, or are utilized in a process. Each also consists of systems and subsystems.

A successful transformation system consists of multiple levels of subsystems, similar to a transportation system, such as an automobile. To move forward, the automobile requires subsystems such as a driver to operate the system, an engine to generate power, fuel to power the engine, tires to provide traction for forward movement, and a planned route to the destination, among other essential components. There are controls, sensors, warning lights, navigation systems, and other subsystems that collect and analyze information from the transportation system to support the management of sublevel processes during operation.

Similarly, the Salvarcar facility required a transformation system with a governing body to lead it, an engine consistently providing power, fuel to sustain the engine, people to generate momentum for progress, and plans with clear goals for the transformation system to follow.

This book examines the transformation system developed by the Salvarcar team, analyzing the components of the sublevel systems, including their inputs, processes, outputs, and the tools, training, and actions implemented to achieve significant transformational results. Since all systems share the same foundational elements, the information here applies to any area of life that requires transformation. These concepts proved effective for Salvarcar and will be valuable for any organization pursuing transformation, employee empowerment, and cultural change.

CHAPTER 2

Systems and the Engine of Transformation

Let's discuss what a system is, what it contains, and what it delivers.

- A system is a group of interconnected processes, components, and elements that work together to produce an output, perform a function, or achieve a specific goal. Here are a few examples of systems: transportation, manufacturing, information and communication, ecosystems, food delivery, and more.
- A system contains raw materials, utilities, air, buildings, people, machinery, equipment, processes, culture, communication, training, and other relevant items. The list is extensive.
- A system provides everything needed to survive and thrive. One system may produce output that another system uses as input for its process. A higher-level system might have several layers of subsystems that provide the inputs required for it to operate, as does an automobile or the human body.

The Engine of Transformation (EOT) must continually operate within an organization to drive positive transformation. An EOT is not a methodology but a process that generates lasting change and can be utilized within any system or subsystem. There are three sections of the EOT, each supported by its own tools, methods, measurements, and processes. All three sections interact synergistically, with their inputs and outputs mutually reinforcing one another. The three sections are Analysis, Innovation, and Process Control. Please watch for the EOT's impact as the Salvarcar story unfolds. Figure 2.1 illustrates the EOT and the interactions of its sections.

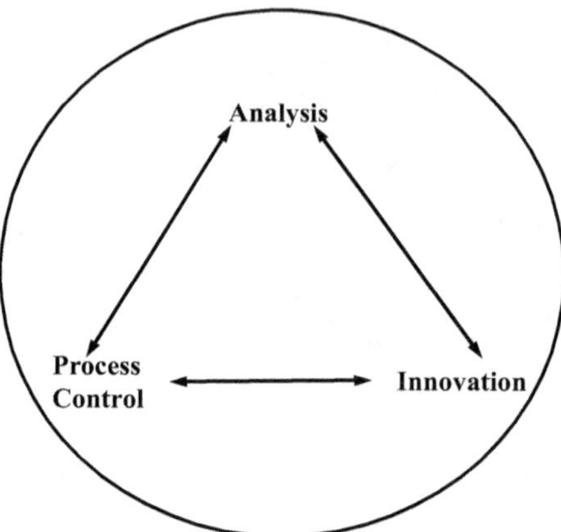

Figure 2.1 The Engine of Transformation

Analysis

The EOT starts with analysis. Transformation depends on data, measurements, and analysis. This subsystem encompasses all the tools, methods, and processes necessary to gather and analyze data, providing the information required to power decisions and actions. Information surrounds us in many different formats. The challenge is to identify and determine if the information is useful, accurate, and complete.

In today's world, almost anything can be measured. Some organizations attempt to do just that and often get lost in the process. It is best to have a few key performance indicators (KPIs) that capture a broad range of inclusivity and to focus on them. These KPIs may be at the system or subsystem level, depending on the context, but they must be inclusive and accurate for the measures being used. If a KPI or measurement is insufficiently inclusive and critical data are excluded from its calculation, suboptimal decisions may result. Examples of this will be highlighted during the review of the Salvarcar case study.

Many organizations currently use various tools to gather and analyze information. Organizations should select those that best fit their needs. When researching systems and their components for transformation and improvement opportunities, there are specific tools that are fundamental, easy to use, and powerful. These will be discussed in Chapter 5.

Innovation

The second section encompasses all the tools, methods, training, and processes employed to generate and realize innovations, including research, imagination, design, and the development of new processes to achieve desired outcomes.

As a young industrial engineering graduate from Arizona State University, I worked for Hughes Aircraft in Tucson, Arizona. The division I worked for was called the Missile Systems Group. To me, Hughes was an engineer's paradise. Almost anything an engineer could imagine and pursue related to new technology and manufacturing innovation was permitted. Money appeared to be limitless.

I was surprised by the ease of obtaining resources, so I inquired about Hughes Aircraft's philosophy on capital expenditures. The reply has given me a lot to think about ever since. It was,

> Hughes has almost unlimited capital funds for innovative engineering development. They rarely censor the imagination of engineers. The company tracks expenditures and understands that approximately 75 percent of the capital expenditures will never make sufficient returns to pay for the expenditures, 15 percent of the projects break even, 7 percent make lots of money for the company for many years; but what the company is after is the remaining 3 percent of expenditures which change the world and have made the company what it is today.

We can all name individuals whose innovations have transformed the world. Here are just a few well-known innovators: Thomas Edison, Steve Jobs, Nikola Tesla, Bill Gates, Elon Musk, Jeff Bezos, Benjamin Franklin, Leonardo Da Vinci, Alexander Graham Bell, Orville and Wilbur Wright, and Galileo Galilei. There are many more. What do they all have in common? Each filled an unfilled need, an opportunity to change the world. Each started in their present state, imagined a future state, and innovated a process to achieve it; then they followed the process to realize the future, adapting as needed along the way.

In the Gene Wilder movie version of *Willy Wonka & the Chocolate Factory*, Wonka sings an epochal song, "Pure Imagination," written by Leslie Bricusse and Anthony Newley.[1] Fragments from the song read, "There is no life I know to compare with pure imagination. Living there, you'll be free if you truly wish to be … Anything you want to, do it. Wanna change the world? There's nothing to it."

I have always loved that song. To me, it sets the stage for developing innovative and creative solutions to any situation in which one seeks to move from one state to a future improved state. Wonka also quoted the beginning of Arthur O'Shaughnessy's "Ode,"[2] which states: "We are the music makers, and we are the dreamers of dreams…."

O'Shaughnessy's Ode goes on to speak to some of the great accomplishments of humankind. Is this not what we as humans do? We examine the current state of life, work, and society, and then envision what it could be. We imagine what could be, then we create the music or make a plan, and then work that plan to get there. Maybe Wonka is right? We are the dreamers of dreams and the music makers, and pure imagination and innovation bridge the gap between the two.

Gary Mack stated the same sentiment in his book *Mind Gym*: "It is said that extraordinary people live their lives backward. They create a future, and then they live into it."[3]

The concepts mentioned by Mack, O'Shaughnessy, and Wonka are interconnected. Let us combine their thoughts into a three-phase approach for innovation: understand the current state, imagine a future state, and bridge the two with innovation.

Understand the Current State

To determine when a system's current state requires transformation, data are gathered, reviewed, and compared against a standard or specification (real or imagined). The current state of the system is then identified as deficient in some way. At this point, pause and consider a few questions:

- Standards, specifications, or expectations—Are they accurate, clearly articulated, and attainable?

- Gathered Data, Measurements, or Information—Is the information collected accurate? How is this assessed? Have all steps of the gathering process been confirmed?
- What elements of the current process or system require transformation?
- What are the underlying causes of the gap between expectations and the current state?

Imagine a Future State

If you had a magic wand and could wave it to create your ideal dream future system, what would it look like? Write down at least the following:

- List in detail the future results you desire. Yes, provide specific details. If we can imagine it, we can do it. What's the dream?
- Establish a new standard, specification, or expectation for future results.
- Do the desired results require innovative changes to the current system, or does the entire system need replacing?

Innovate a Process

Let us innovate, design, and build a process that can take us from our current system state to our imagined future state, or as close to it as possible. Imagination is not innovation, but innovation requires imagination to be successful. Selecting and applying a suitable transformation structure can accelerate the innovation process.

Just as water cannot be drawn from an empty well, innovation relies on knowledge bases found in individuals, groups, companies, industries, and other information sources scattered around the world. Understanding the extent of knowledge needed would be beneficial when innovating to solve a specific problem.

Genrich Altshuller was a pioneering figure in the field of technical innovation. He outlined three steps to improve systems: decompose a system into its basic elements; divide the system into subsystems; and begin analysis at the subsystem level, where innovation is required, then rebuild the system from the bottom up. He also stated that, over time, continued innovation will gradually move a system toward the ideal.[4]

No organization, product, process, or system is ever truly finished. The world constantly changes. Technology advances, people grow, and obsolescence occurs. The future will always be promising for those who can imagine, innovate, adapt, and avoid getting stuck in the present. Everyone can innovate, and many do. Understanding the information in this chapter can support the innovation process at every level.

Process Control

The third section of the EOT is process control. Generating a new output through innovation requires establishing and controlling processes to ensure the desired output is consistently achieved. Systems are filled with processes. Processes are designed and built during the imagination and innovation part of the EOT. Processes are the activities we perform throughout the day. Processes produce outputs that are part of systems. Processes are everywhere in all organizations. Given this, a key to controlling and transforming systems is effective process control.

Thomas A. Little, PhD, outlined the 10 steps for controlling a process: clear specification, measurement, process capability, inspection plan, data collection, out-of-control plan, documentation, training, database, and auditing.[5] The majority of companies perform well on steps 5 through 10. Most process failures usually occur during steps 1 to 4. We now discuss these steps.

1. **Clear Specification**—May include product specifications, drawings, standards, desired outcomes, work instructions, or objectives to be achieved. One of the primary factors contributing to process failures or quality issues is the presence of unclear, imprecise, or incorrect specifications. Take the time to ensure the specifications are clear, precise, and understood by all parties involved in designing and operating the process.
2. **Measurement**—Specify the instrument to be used, the measurement method or process to follow, determine what to measure, and conduct a gauge repeatability and reproducibility (Gauge R&R) study,

which is a statistical method used to evaluate the capability and variation of the measurement system. It identifies if the variation is caused by the part's dimensions or by the measurement system.

3. **Process Capability**—This step is crucial because it determines the overall quality of the process output. Ensure the process can meet the specifications with a five-sigma capability or higher, meaning that 99.98 percent of all process outputs meet the specifications. This involves conducting a capability study that includes measuring and comparing results against specifications. If the process cannot meet these standards, adjust the process, method, or specifications until the required capability is achieved. Innovation is not complete until a capable process is developed! Treat this as a fixed rule and follow it without exception. Adhering to this principle will prevent countless future issues.
4. **Create Inspection Plans**—Inspection plans should be developed after evaluating process capability to prevent over-inspection, under-inspection, and inefficiency. Too often, inspection criteria are established before conducting a process capability study. Consequently, these criteria remain in place during production, which is a poor practice. Instead, align the inspection plan with the actual data obtained from a process capability study once the process is operational. Additionally, determine who will conduct the inspections and how frequently they will be performed.
5. **Data Collection**—Design the format, medium, and process to use for data collection.
6. **Out of Control Plan**—Decide who takes action when a process produces out-of-specification output. What actions should be taken? What information needs to be recorded and where?
7. **Documentation**—Work instructions, procedures, and other essential details must be documented.
8. **Training**—Train on the process documentation. Determine who, when, how, and where to train. Certify the people being trained before allowing them to work in the process.
9. **Database**—Identify where data, measurements, and documentation should be stored and backed up. Ensure access is available for future analysis.

10. **Periodic Audits**—Ensure that processes, procedures, and measurement methodologies are being followed. Determine who will perform the audits, as well as the frequency and format.

Chapter Summary

- Systems require an EOT to achieve their full potential.
- An EOT is composed of three sections: Analysis, Innovation, and Process Control.
- An EOT requires accurate, inclusive data to power its engine.
- Innovation is occurring every day, all around us, in every aspect and activity.
- There are three phases to innovation: Understanding the current system state, imagining a future system state, and innovating a process to get from here to there.
- A process to facilitate innovation involves breaking down a system into subsystems and basic elements, then effecting change at those levels and rebuilding the system.
- Over time, any system is driven to ideality through continued innovation.
- Imagination is not innovation, but innovation requires imagination.
- Effective process control is a critical component of a successful EOT.

CHAPTER 3

Where to Begin

When faced with a complex and challenging assignment, various questions may arise in one's mind. Some are positive, while others are negative. Some might consider an assignment impossible and create a lengthy list of reasons to support that view. Others may believe that completing the assignment is feasible but not within the given time frame, which leads them to compile a list of reasons to support their position. Much of this negative thinking stems from fear, perhaps a fear of failure?

Growing up, I loved playing all kinds of sports. I spent most of my free time participating in whatever sport was in season. Sports involve performance psychology, emotional regulation techniques, and repetitive skill practice. In my youth, coaches were often viewed as great performance psychologists. They shared motivational sayings during practices to inspire players to strive for improvement. Here are two that have stuck with me over the years:

> Whether you believe you can do a thing or not, you are right. (Henry Ford)
>
> That which we persist in doing becomes easier for us to do—not that the nature of the thing is changed, but that our power to do is increased. (Heber J. Grant)

We were also well acquainted with a frequently misattributed 1960 study conducted by L. Verdelle Clark at Wayne State University, titled "Effect of Mental Practice on the Development of a Certain Motor Skill." In this study, Clark selected 144 high school students, with 36 from four different high schools. These 36 students were divided into three groups of 12 each. The first group consisted of varsity basketball players, the second group included junior varsity basketball players, and the third group comprised novice basketball players. At each high school, all three groups met together and were instructed in a specific shooting technique known as "the Pacific Coast one-hand foul shot." Some instructions given to the students are quoted.

> They then read printed information on the technique for shooting the Pacific Coast one-handed foul shot. The next step was for subjects to position themselves on a line facing the instructor, who gave them instructions in the shooting technique to be employed during the experiment. The subjects were asked to pose through the sequence of positions of body and limb, without a basketball, as the instructor described and demonstrated them. **Knowing**, specificity of motions; **seeing**, self and instructor while posing through the successive positions; and **feeling**, kinesthetic sensations with eyes both opened and closed, were emphasized.[6]

Clark then repeated the entire above process with each person physically holding and using a basketball. Each player then took 25 free throws, with an instructor monitoring and giving pointers to improve form and technique. The original instructions were repeated, and then all players took an additional 25 free throws, with the results recorded to establish the baseline percentages for free throws made.

Notice the emphasis that Clark placed on mastering the technique, form, and motion: reading how to do it, seeing how to do it, and then practicing the effort, both with and without the ball in their hands. Next, they practiced shooting the ball while receiving feedback on their form and technique. This sequence is a prime example of effective training methods.

The varsity, junior varsity, and novice players were mixed and divided into two groups at each high school. The groups were instructed not to discuss anything regarding the specific instructions given to them with the other group. The experiment was conducted over 14 days.

Group 1 was instructed to practice physically every day by shooting five warm-up free throws, followed by 25 free throws, and recording the results, with no additional instructions given. Group 2 was the experimental group. This group received written instructions for the mental visualization practice technique. They were to read the mental visualization technique instructions daily at the beginning of their mental practice. They were to visualize taking five warm-up shots and then visualize taking and making 25 free throws for a score but did not physically shoot a basketball.

After 14 days, the groups reconvened for the final testing. They all took 25 warm-up shots and then 25 shots for scoring. The combined results of the percent improvement for the four high schools were as follows.

Student type	Physical practice	Mental practice only
Varsity	16%	15%
Junior varsity	24%	23%
Novice	44%	26%

A few comments about the results will be helpful as we proceed with this book. When analyzing data, an important question to ask is, "Does the data make sense?" In this case, it does; the improvement is directional, from the varsity group to the novice group, which is expected. Let us use the varsity and novice results to illustrate critical trends that may help advance understanding of potential for improvement.

First, a player with a higher skill level, such as an 80 percent free-throw shooter, has less potential for improvement than a novice player who is still learning the game and has a 25 percent free-throw percentage. This implies that the 80 percent shooter could improve by 16 percent to 92.8 percent, which would be an excellent free-throw percentage. In contrast, the novice player would show greater progress, increasing by 44 percent to achieve a 36 percent success rate—a notable improvement, though still a relatively low free-throw shooting percentage. There remains considerable room for improvement.

The same applies when executing business transformations. Some operations may already have a higher level of skill than others. Some may have advanced procedures in key areas, so learning new techniques and implementing them with precision will lead to improvement. However, there may be fewer opportunities to capture than in an operation that has not practiced and implemented many well-known industry practices. Much like the basketball example, there is a significant opportunity for improvement, given the substantial gap between their current state and their potential.

Second, more skilled basketball players who visualized the mechanics and imagined the ball going through the net achieved nearly the same improvement as those who engaged in actual physical practice. This proved effective for those who had been shooting a basketball for years. However, for novice players with little experience, physical practice was more crucial for enhancing their shooting skills than merely visualizing the techniques, given their limited background. This aligns with the Heber J. Grant quote above, "That which we persist in doing becomes easier for us to do..."

The key to this study was that players were not left to develop their own process or method for achieving the desired improvement; coaches taught them a specific process and then practiced it both physically and mentally.

Knowing, Seeing, and Feeling—These concepts have been applied in sports, education, and business to achieve higher rates of performance improvement, particularly through a combination of physical practice, mental imagery, and effective coaching. Watching the Olympics, you will see many athletes with their eyes closed, envisioning the competition and their performance before they take the stage. Some even perform visible physical motions as part of this imagery review.

Sport psychologists teach that one strategy to enhance performance is regulating the emotion of fear. The opposite of fear is often defined as knowledge, understanding, and learning. Indeed, a fear of the unknown or chaos, especially in unfamiliar or disorganized situations, can lead to anxiety or paralyze thought and action if left unchecked.

Coaches dedicate hours to teaching, training, and practicing skills, as well as game situations, while encouraging athletes to execute basic skills quickly and accurately. They aim to enhance strength, speed, conditioning, and teamwork to improve performance and triumph over opponents. Consistent practice fosters habits and muscle memory, promoting an automatic response during competition. Learning, knowledge, and developed behaviors can help eliminate fear. This principle is also applicable in the business world.

To transform a company, it is essential to equip the organization with the necessary skills, processes, and techniques. The organization must also see examples of success using the latest skills, methods, and processes. Then, they should practice these while receiving expert feedback on their performance, utilizing the newly acquired knowledge.

Following the basketball experiment model, an organization, company, department, or team can transform its current performance into its highest potential. Emphasize that the process of improving understanding is ongoing and the journey is never truly finished. The primary focus is not on competing with and defeating the competition but on reaching full potential. Competitive results will naturally improve as we do so.

So, where do we go from here? When facing a challenge or an ambitious goal, instead of wasting time and energy listing reasons why the task can't be finished within the given timeframe and dwelling on it—which could lead to negative visualization, despair, or even failure—focus your mental energy on answering the question, "What do we need to do to accomplish the task in the time allowed?" Take some time to consider, imagine, and visualize the steps necessary for success. Then learn the required skills, take action, and accomplish it. This closely aligns with Clark's comments on "knowing" (knowledge), "seeing" (examples of learning techniques to use), and "feeling" (hands-on experience of getting it done).

We will now follow the Salvarcar team as they organize to begin their transformation to reach their full potential. In this case, the transformation of the Salvarcar facility and its entire system began with four key points: organizing a Transformation Council, communicating the task, and reviewing and selecting KPIs to focus on.

Organize a Transformation Council

A transformation system requires a driver that provides direction, goals, and leadership to all those working within the system being transformed. In this case, the driver is referred to as the Transformation Council. The Transformation Council is the leadership group responsible for overseeing the resources and personnel across the entire site. This group is responsible for decision making and for managing all actions undertaken, typically comprising the site leadership staff. To be successful, this responsibility cannot be delegated to another group. In this case, the council's leader was the head of Western Hemisphere Manufacturing. The council members included the operations manager, quality manager, human resource manager, both production planners, safety, health, and environmental (SHE) engineer, engineering manager, finance controller, maintenance manager, materials manager (responsible for purchasing, warehouse, and customs), and the head of the Western Hemisphere's administrative assistant. This leadership group was accountable for the site's performance. They were the ones who directly led the significant transformations that would occur.

Communicate the Task

A short story highlighting the importance of communication when major changes are planned may help clarify this point. A few years before the Salvarcar story, I worked for a large cable and connector company serving as the director of operations for Mexico. Part of my responsibilities was relocating the labor-intensive manufacturing footprint of 11 small facilities from the United States and Canada to a single 230,000 sq. ft. facility in Mexico. After the company's executive council officially announced a facility relocation to employees, I was tasked with visiting the facility to present the transfer schedule to management, organizing a bi-plant transfer team, and managing all aspects of the transfer. All transfers went smoothly except one, the Hazelton, Pennsylvania, facility.

The day before I traveled to Hazelton, I received a phone call from the executive responsible for that facility. He requested that I meet with the entire plant staff, and not just the leadership team, to explain the transfer schedule. This was a deviation from the norm, but I did not think much of it and agreed to do it.

At the facility, I first met with the plant manager to discuss the day's events, then with plant employees. As I presented the details of the plant's relocation and shutdown, it became clear that this was the first time most in the room had heard that the plant was being shut down and relocated. There were many questions about layoff benefits, why this action was necessary, the dates by which each person would be let go, and other important matters that should have already been addressed by the responsible executive and HR department many days before I arrived. I stated as much to those in attendance and promised to call the corporate office later that day to send someone to address these issues. I informed them that each would have a personalized plan generated, including layoff timing, benefits, retraining opportunities, employment assistance, and more. The meeting was then dismissed.

After the meeting, I went to a small conference room with the plant manager and his staff for a working lunch. Five minutes into lunch, a knock on the door was heard, and the plant manager was called out of our meeting. Soon, he returned and excused everyone from the room except me. He informed me that two workers had gone to their trucks, retrieved their hunting rifles, and were waiting in the wooded area near the front exit of the facility, and that they were going to shoot me when I left the building and headed to my car. He asked me to gather my belongings and immediately leave with him through the back loading docks, where his car was parked, and he would drive me from the facility while I lay on the back seat floor. We would exit the parking lot through the parking lot opposite the wooded area. My rental car would be left in the parking lot, and someone else would return it later at the end of the day. Only the plant manager knew where I was staying for the night, so I would be safe at the hotel.

We immediately left with all six foot five inches of me hiding on the rear seat floor of a medium-sized car. The escape was successful, and a great tragedy was avoided. Soon, all employees received their personalized information, and they settled down. Over the subsequent four months, the plant was successfully relocated.

For years, I was unsure if the possible assassination situation was real or fabricated to get me out of the facility. Eighteen years after the fact, I met two individuals who were at the Hazelton facility that day; they informed me that it was real and that two men were indeed waiting with their hunting rifles for me to leave the facility.

The night after the escape and on the plane ride home the next morning, I reflected on what had happened and decided there must be a better way to communicate important changes to employees. Communication should never be omitted; it should be carefully developed and presented to all employees involved in the change. Below is the communication plan used with the Salvarcar staff. It may be useful as an example.

When communicating critical or strategic information, people like to know the following:

- What action is being requested?
- Why is it important and necessary?

- Why is it important to take action now?
- What role does each individual have in achieving the action?
- What occurs if the action is not taken?
- What is the timeline?
- How does the change impact each individual?

A recurring meeting notice was sent to the site leadership group to meet each morning at 9:00 a.m. The meeting was intended to serve as both a staff meeting to review daily metrics and discuss actions based on those metrics, and a forum for transformation-related discussions.

By the time of the first morning meeting, information was prepared for discussion regarding each of the six questions:

1. **What is being requested?** The site's operational costs were excessively high, consistently exceeding the monthly budget. The goal was to develop and implement a plan to reduce operational costs and recurring expenses over the next six months, along with a roadmap for ongoing improvements. Current operating expenses were mainly categorized into two groups: standard material usage, which accounted for 44 percent of all operating costs, and other expenses, which represented 56 percent. Although the company president did not provide a target, achieving a significant and permanent transformation that could lower nonmaterial recurring operating costs by 30 percent or more was necessary.
2. **Why is it important and necessary?** The patents on the high-performance industrial gloves were set to expire in July of that year (six months away), allowing competition to enter the marketplace and threaten our dominant position. To remain competitive, we needed to reduce the standard cost of our products and extend patent protection through innovative changes to our product lines.
3. **Why should we take action now?** Costs needed to be lowered before the patents expired, customer contracts ended, and competition could ramp up. The company estimated that it would take the competition approximately 12 to 18 months from the expiration of the patents to enter the marketplace.

4. **What role does each individual have in achieving the action?** Each leadership group member was responsible for developing and implementing improvement ideas throughout the plant. Each manager would be accountable for training their team members, maintaining a positive and can-do attitude, and collaborating with other managers and employees across all facility areas to ensure success in this effort. The company sought substantial transformations of existing processes and opportunities for continuous improvement. The bigger, the better. Everything was a candidate for change, so think big.
5. **What occurs if the action is not taken?** Our competitive product lines would be relocated to sister plants in Southeast Asian countries with lower labor and operating costs. Everyone in the facility would be affected if the product lines needed to be moved.
6. **What is the timeline?** Six months must be allocated to demonstrate significant progress or to be well into the implementation phase of the transformation plans. The definition of "good improvement" was not yet available. That determination would be made after a high-level initial investigation into what could be achieved.

A candid, straightforward, and practical discussion ensued regarding all six items mentioned. The financial information and the expiration of the patents somewhat surprised the staff. This information had not previously been shared with the site leadership team.

Review Measurements

Salvarcar had been measuring its glove-knitting system using high-level KPIs. When examining KPIs, it is beneficial to consider four key questions: How is the KPI calculated? Where does the raw data originate? Is the data a subset of a primary, more inclusive KPI? Can the data be manipulated to provide a false reality?

Data for a KPI should come from the financial and enterprise resource planning (ERP) databases. This is the same information reported to corporate, which everyone uses and maintains to run the company, and it represents the most accurate data available. Too often, people create standalone databases to track KPIs or savings from improvements. Savings must be reflected in the company's financial statements to validate their authenticity and legitimacy. Too often, individuals report saving half a person, 20 minutes here and 30 minutes there as savings, but no changes appear in the official financial reports! Those types of savings may not be genuine if the time saved is not utilized productively to have a positive impact on the financial statements.

Choosing KPIs is a critical function to get right. Don't go KPI crazy! Not everything can be changed at once, so be selective and prioritize. Additional KPIs can always be developed and tracked later.

The KPIs being tracked by the knitting company were mentioned in Chapter 1. The team spent several days gathering sufficient data to understand all the KPIs, potential savings, improvements, and the implementation speed for each saving opportunity. One example, along with answers to the four questions from above, is included from the team's KPI review.

- **Scrap rate: 14 percent**
  - 14 percent of 44 percent of raw material costs amounted to a significant sum, representing 6.2 percent of total operational expenses.
  - **How is this KPI calculated?** The standard cost for all parts scrapped in a day is divided by the standard cost of all products produced on the same day. The standard cost was made up of material, labor, and overhead for each part number. The material consisted of yarn and thread. Some gloves underwent post-process screen printing to add material to the palms or backs.
  - **Where does the raw data originate?** The quality department enters scrapped material into the ERP system via a scrap ticket.
  - **Is this data a subset of a primary, more inclusive KPI?** Yes, it is included in the material variance cost, as reported in the monthly financial statements. In this case, the two components of material variance were scrap from scrap tickets and inventory cycle count variances, which consisted of material issued to the floor that did not return to the warehouse as finished goods, or missing finished goods from the warehouse.

- **Can the data be manipulated to provide a false reality?** Yes, it can. All that is required is not to write a scrap ticket; the scrap will default to the inventory cycle count material variance.

Therefore, a KPI for scrap alone is inadequate. The roll-up level of material variance should serve as the site-level KPI. All materials used but not shipped would be included in this category, resulting in a variance for all materials issued to manufacturing, with no manipulations of this number.

Select Focus KPIs

During the KPI discussion, three key process areas emerged as potential opportunities for improvement. These included:

1. **Scrap and Inventory Cycle Count**: These contribute to material variance, so we will refer to them as material variance moving forward. material variance potentially accounts for 20.3 percent of all annual recurring expenses—an unusually high amount.
2. **Efficiency:** At 45 percent, efficiency appears to be an area that requires significant improvement.
   a. Most of the manpower was spent operating knitting machines. The data indicated that the knitting machines operated for only 50 percent of the scheduled time. Other operations, such as overedge sewing and screen printing, demand constant attention, making them inherently more efficient. However, with one operator managing 11 knitting machines, the efficiency may indicate the machines are underperforming due to various issues. This presents a great opportunity.
   b. The facility had 1,320 knitting machines divided across 30 work cells. Each knitting machine produced one pair of gloves every six minutes. The facility operated two shifts, with not all machines producing the same products and not all scheduled to run weekly. If they could all be scheduled to run, that would amount to approximately 1.3 million pairs per day. There must be a significant opportunity for transformation here! Perhaps at

least 1 million pairs could be produced each week? Currently, the plant averages only 500K pairs per week.

3. **Cycle Time:** A cycle time of three weeks seems long, considering that one pair of gloves comes off a machine every six minutes and 1,320 knitting machines are in operation. There is no reason for a work order to take three weeks to produce. It should take no more than a day or even just a few hours. The floor was cluttered with materials. This situation should be examined further, and it may not be necessary to schedule three separate processes (knitting, overedge, screen printing). Additionally, reducing the three weeks of material currently staged as WIP on the floor would yield significant one-time savings. There should also be a considerable reduction in indirect labor hours associated with moving, counting, scheduling, and handling excess material. Often, material is missing, so streamlining the process should help address these issues as well. Let's get leaner!
4. **All else**—The transformation team decided that the other measurements might be connected to the three chosen areas mentioned above, and that by transforming those process areas, other KPIs would likely improve. This idea seemed reasonable, and due to limited resources, the decision was made to prioritize the three measurements mentioned.

Chapter Summary

- Focus on what needs to be done to achieve the goal, not on why something cannot be done.
- If we think we can or cannot do something, we are likely correct.
- There are three steps in learning skills: "knowing" (knowledge); "seeing" (examples of learning techniques to use); "feeling" (hands-on experience in getting it done).
- Where to begin Transformation: Organize a Transformation Council, communicate the task at hand, review KPIs in detail, and select focus KPIs for improvement.

CHAPTER 4

Project Teams

Those who provide the traction and momentum for a transformation system are the people participating in project teams. To build effective project teams, a framework must be in place to select, train, monitor, and support team members. There are eight components to the team structure process: Transformation Council, Project Selection, Team Charter, Team Members, Kickoff, Team Training, Status Reporting, and Team Closure Meeting.

Transformation Council

The Transformation Council facilitates transformation and cultural change. Without their efforts to work with individuals at all levels of the organization, success may not occur at the desired pace and scale, making it impossible to achieve rapid transformation and cultural change. As previously stated, the site management staff constitutes the Transformation Council, chaired by the site manager.

Project Selection

The Transformation Council is responsible for project selection and determining the key deliverables for each project. The Council reviews system metrics and KPIs and selects projects to undertake. This function was discussed in depth in Chapter 3.

Just a brief reminder of a couple of key points. First, resources are limited; focus only on the most critical and impactful opportunities. Second, as with the first point, it can take as much time and resources to resolve a minor, complex issue that does not significantly impact finances as it does to pursue a substantial, high-value opportunity. Therefore, choose wisely which projects to undertake. An example of a project selection guide is found in Figure 4.1.

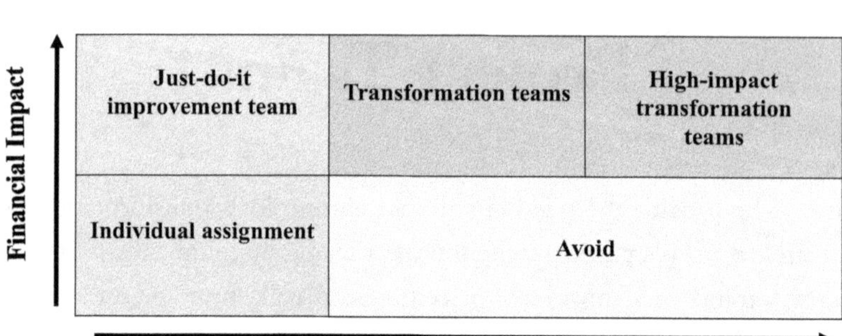

Figure 4.1 Project selection guide

Team Charter

A staff manager will be selected to champion each team. Part of the champion's responsibilities is to develop a team charter and present it to the Transformation Council for approval.

The purpose of a team charter is to provide clear specifications for the project to be undertaken. As with the Clark free-throw experiment, the charter will be read at the beginning of the kickoff meeting and at the start of each project team meeting. Doing this helps focus the team on the project's purpose and goals, keeping the team on track. A charter can prevent the confusion that sometimes occurs when only verbal instructions are given. A clear team charter will include, at a minimum, the following sections of information:

- **Name of the project**
- **Kickoff date**
- **Champion**—The staff manager responsible for the team's success. This person will follow up with the team leader at least weekly to ensure progress is being made and that resources are provided as needed to advance the team.
- **KPIs Impacted**—Identify the KPI impacted by this project and how calculated.

- **Current State**—Clearly articulate the issue and the opportunity for improvement. Explain the process or system to be transformed. The information should be monetized and explain how the current state impacts the financial reports.
- **Imagined Future State**—Clearly describe the desired future state. Outline the potential improvements that can be achieved. This should include the measurement specifications, how they are calculated, the data sources, the starting measurement, and the goals for the final measurements. The expected timeframe for achieving the goals is typically three to six months.
- **Project Scope**—Clearly define the project's scope, recommend training to be offered, and provide other specific instructions from the Council for the team. The scope is especially crucial when multiple teams address different aspects of a significant opportunity.
- **Team Members**—All team members are privately asked if they would like to participate in a team. Provide details about the team and outline their responsibilities. Participation must be voluntary to foster synergy among the team members. The team leader and up to six other team members are identified. With rare exceptions, teams should not exceed seven people. A team of three to five members is ideal. The Transformation Council ensures that the appropriate resources from various departments are allocated to the team to enable its success. As the team progresses, adjustments to team members can be made as necessary. Outside resource individuals can also be included in the team member section. A resource is someone who possesses critical information essential to the team's success, such as an area expert, and only attends meetings when invited; however, they can be contacted at any time to provide information and assistance. Such resources are not counted toward the team member head count.

Team charters may take any reasonable and desired format as determined by the Transformation Council. They may include additional sections and information beyond what is mentioned above. The key point is that a team should be able to read the charter and understand their goal, how it will be measured, the available opportunities, who their team members are, and the completion date. Clear specifications are essential and the most critical aspect of a team project, ensuring there is no confusion about how to proceed.

Team Members

The team's purpose is to achieve its goal. The highest probability of success on complex projects is achieved with a diverse, balanced team. The backgrounds, experiences, skills, and thought processes of a diverse group differ. Consider selecting employees from various groups, such as older employees, younger employees, males, females, engineers, HR personnel, hourly workers, and salaried staff, to participate together. Sometimes, people with little knowledge of the project subject have important insights that others might not have considered.

One interesting commonality I've noticed in my experience is that when a group is composed entirely of the same type of employees (e.g., age, sex, education), they often struggle with problem-solving and generating innovative solutions. This pattern has been consistent across all global locations and cultural contexts. I frequently reflect on this phenomenon and have asked those being trained why it happens. The response suggests that schooling, experiences, and thought processes are very similar across all team members when the group is composed solely of the same type of employee. As a result, their view of the world tends to be overly simple and uniform. The best performers, however, tend to be those in diverse groups. When working on transformation projects, assembling a diverse team is crucial.

Two real-world examples from the Salvarcar plant illustrate the value of a transformation team working on a project to improve uptime on glove-knitting machines. At the time of the project's kickoff, the facility had only male engineers, maintenance workers, and operators running the machines. The transformation team included a female HR employee and a female quality control employee to achieve a more balanced representation. Some male team members complained about including individuals who lacked experience with operating and repairing knitting machines. After much discussion, the team agreed to have a more diverse group.

It turned out that one of the major downtime issues was machines stopping when the yarn and thread ran out. When a spool of yarn runs out, a sensor automatically stops the machine to prevent empty needles from creating holes in the glove. When the yarn from a new spool is tied to the end of the loose yarn from the empty spool, the machine can be restarted. Since operators managed 11 machines each, a stopped knitting machine would remain down until the operator noticed it was no longer operational.

The engineers wanted to install a light on each machine to signal when it had stopped. This was a practical solution implemented. The quality control employee explained that everyone who sews knows to stop the sewing machine before the spool runs out, tie the new spool of thread to the old one, and restart the machine. They also understand that higher-capacity spools are available, reducing the need to replace empty spools as frequently. The application requires purchasing double-capacity spools of yarn and inspecting their status while the machines are running. When the yarn begins to run low, unspool the remaining yarn, tie the end of the old yarn to the new spool, and wind the unspooled yarn onto the new spool. This approach ensures the machine never has to stop. This second solution removed machine stoppages caused by that specific downtime issue and was also implemented.

The example illustrates the importance of considering diverse thoughts, experiences, and worldviews when evaluating opportunities. Team members can exchange ideas, leading to a synergistic solution that is often better than the sum of their individual contributions.

The team's composition can either contribute to or detract from achieving a project goal successfully. Take the time to ensure teams are diverse and consist of seven members or fewer.

Kickoff Meeting

Kicking off a project team is a 10-minute event. Before the kickoff, team members should have already spoken with their manager and have a copy of the team charter. The leader has been selected and trained on his responsibilities. The team will now meet with the entire Transformation Council to discuss the project's significance to the company. Having the entire Council present underscores the project's importance and enables all team members to interact with the site leadership team. Being handpicked to participate in such an important team is a significant honor. The short kickoff meeting agenda can be as follows:

- **Introductions**—The chairperson of the Transformation Council introduces the Council members and says a few words about the honor and importance of being selected to participate in this team. He reviews the project team's expectations and the status-reporting process, then turns the floor over to the council member, who will be the project team's champion.
- **Present the charter and the project team members**—The champion quickly reviews the charter and introduces the project team members. He emphasizes the importance of meeting at least weekly, sending meeting minutes to the Transformation Council, and actively participating in team meetings to address action items. An opportunity to ask relevant questions is provided to all present.
- **The Transformation Council leaves** the room, and the champion and the project team stay for their first meeting. The champion can provide team training during this first meeting.

Team Training

The legendary UCLA basketball coach John Wooden won 10 NCAA National Championships across 12 years. He is considered "The Wizard of Westwood" and the greatest college basketball coach of the twentieth century. One of his many famous quotes is, "Do not let what you cannot do interfere with what you can do."[7]

This is excellent advice when working with project teams. There is never enough time or training for a team to know every tool that could help with their project. Trained resources are selected to help a team succeed. These resources have been trained in the essential tools needed for improvement. There is no reason to delay kicking off the team due to a lack of toolbox training. Let these trained resources support the teams as they progress through the transformation process. Every person solves problems in life and at work, so everyone has some level of ability. Get the team organized and moving forward. Training can be provided during team meetings, as the team works on their project, and when they need a specific tool from the toolbox.

In Chapter 5, we will discuss some of the basic tools that should be in the project team's toolbox. For now, we are getting the team moving forward. As part of the team initiation process, which may occur during the first team meeting, there should be some basic training on what a team is, how it operates, and how each team member is expected to participate in the team, how to carry out effective meetings, and how to take and disseminate team minutes to the team and the Transformation Council members.

Remember the steps of training presented by Clark to those participating in the free-throw experiment: **Knowing** (learning the subject), **Seeing** (the knowledge put to use by experts), **Feeling** (using the knowledge). There is also a feedback loop, with an expert helping the performer to use the knowledge correctly. Then, the performer can practice applying the knowledge and imagine using it, accelerating proficiency as the team progresses. The champion meets the need for expert feedback and ensures the team receives all necessary training to succeed.

Status Reporting

Consistently holding status-reporting meetings is a top priority for the Transformation Council. Without this step in the process, project teams slow down their activities, and the projects lose priority to the daily business needs. If a team knows it will report on the status of its action items to the entire Transformation Council every two weeks, the team leader will come prepared. The team leader will want to present well to the leadership staff. Being on a team is a chance to shine and demonstrate one's abilities.

If a team project is sufficiently important to warrant the entire Transformation Council's attendance, it is a significant project for the team to excel at. Having good charters and consistent attendance at the status reporting meeting should produce 80 percent of the expected results from a team. This is the importance of status reporting.

A status meeting should be scheduled for one hour every week. Half of the team leaders attend the weekly meeting one week to present their status. The following week, the other half of the team leaders attend the status meeting to present their updates. This way, each team leader will provide their team's status every two weeks.

The status report agenda is as follows:

- Each team leader is given a maximum of five to seven minutes to present their status.
- Each team leader uses the same format structure for the information (as described below).
- No additional information should be presented other than that which the form solicits.
- The Transformation Council should hold comments and questions until the leader finishes the presentation, then they can ask questions, provide needed direction, modify the charter if needed, provide additional resources and help, and congratulate the leader on their progress.

Six teams can report status at this meeting if required. It is rare for a Transformation Council to have more than ten active key projects underway at once. So, a one-hour time slot should be sufficient for six or fewer teams to provide their status reports and leave time for the Council to discuss other Transformation items of interest.

The "Biweekly Update Report to Transformation Council" contains the following information:

- Project name and date of the presentation. The charter should be presented and quickly reviewed so that all present can recall the current state, opportunities, and future state goals of this team, as well as the team members. This will add focus to the information.
- List and review the activities accomplished that were scheduled to be completed the previous two weeks, as found on the previous Update Report. Then, if additional actions were taken that were not previously scheduled, discuss them as well.
- List and review the activities planned for the next two weeks. Talk about the impact and purpose of the planned activities.

- List and review any risks, barriers, issues, or assistance needed from the Transformation Council. This is an opportunity for the team to identify items that are slowing or stopping progress.
- Lastly, the project metrics are reviewed, and the team leader can project the impact of the actions being taken on future metrics results.
- The status reports should be saved in a database for future reference.

Team Closure Meeting

In this meeting, the entire project team is invited to present their project, from start to finish. This formal slide presentation features pictures, graphs, data, and other visual elements. The team discusses the activities accomplished during each step of the methodology they followed. They present the tools used, the training provided, the results, and the lessons learned. If possible, each team member will provide a portion of the presentation and have the opportunity to speak with the Transformation Council. Once again, the questions are held until the presentation ends.

The presentation should last no more than 30 minutes. The champion is responsible for helping the team understand the presentation format and for reviewing all content and the final presentation before it is presented to the Transformation Council. The presentation and results will be a positive experience for the team members. The final presentation is scheduled only once the champion is satisfied that everything is correct, complete, and well-practiced.

After the presentation, members of the Transformation Council may ask questions on any project-related topic, including participation, methodology, or other relevant areas. They then thank the team, congratulate them on the results, and have refreshments with them.

The team presentation and picture could then be posted on a communication board along with the charter and results. If the organization has a digital social media program, the presentation, pictures, and results can be posted on its website.

Participating as a team member and then as a project team leader is an excellent way to identify and develop future leaders for the company.

Indeed, all the necessary elements are in place to make that happen if properly managed.

Chapter Summary

- A successful transformation system consists of several key components. Each part is essential and has specific goals associated with its function: the Transformation Council, project selection, team charter, team members, team kickoff, team training, status reporting, and team closure.
- Approximately 80 percent of a project's success is associated with following the project team process.
- Basic training on the functionality of a team and each person's responsibility as a team member should be provided during the first team meeting.
- Other team training can be accomplished, as a team moves forward, by an experienced resource assigned to help each team be successful.
- Each team leader reporting to the Transformation Council every two weeks is critical for success and is the number one activity that helps a team reach its project goals.
- It's OK to start a team with minimal training. Train as the team progresses. Remember Wooden's words, "Do not let what you cannot do interfere with what you can do."

CHAPTER 5

Toolbox Tools

Every improvement or transformation system that organizes project teams includes a toolbox of tools that team members can access and use as needed. Organizations can choose which tools to include in their toolbox. Some tools may be complex and require extensive training and experience to operate effectively. Other tools are basic and simple enough that any employee can be quickly taught to use them successfully. It is surprising how much change can be achieved using basic tools. This chapter lists and briefly discusses some commonly used tools. Examples of how these tools are used will appear in the chapters that discuss the innovative process changes the Salvarcar teams implemented during their transformation project work. Additional details on these tools and their usage are available elsewhere for those who desire them.

Brainstorming

Brainstorming is a popular method for sharing ideas. Brainstorming works best when participants have relevant experience and knowledge of the subject under discussion. When done correctly, it quickly generates ideas, potential solutions, and concepts shaped by the participation of everyone present, resulting in outcomes that are often better and more creative than the sum of individual ideas—ideas feed off each other. To work best, a group with diverse talents should be gathered to participate in the brainstorming session. Each individual is allowed to speak freely in turn. All ideas are listed, without censorship, regardless of how outlandish they may seem. If some comments share a similar nature, they are combined into a single concept. Then, a weighted voting system should be used to rank the gathered ideas in order of importance, based on the session's purpose.

Expert Interviews

Interviewing "experts" or "people in the know" is an excellent way to understand how a system works and identify potential causes of problems. Consulting an expert can significantly save time in the investigation process. It's important to distinguish between information within the expert's area of expertise and opinions outside that area. Prepare your questions in advance. They should focus on the how, what, when, where, who, and similar details to collect data for analysis. Additionally, ask the expert who else might be an expert worth interviewing. This approach increases the chances of obtaining accurate information and facts by verifying details with others.

Problem-Solving

When solving problems, most of the time should be dedicated to understanding the issue and its full context; only then can a good, lasting solution be found. Organizations, individuals, and families need to solve problems. Problems are addressed daily. Sometimes, a simple list of questions to ask can be helpful in the problem-solving process. A few straightforward questions can quickly guide thinking toward the root cause.

Usually, these questions are most effective in identifying why something that was working properly no longer functions as intended. Adapt these questions as needed to suit the specific problem being solved:

- When did the issue or defect begin?
- Why is this problem happening now and not before? What changed?
- Where on the part is the defect located? Why is the issue not located elsewhere?
- What percentage of the parts have the issue or defect? Why don't all the parts have the defect or issue?
- What similar part numbers are there that do not have an issue? Why?
- What other part numbers run on the machine or through the process? Do they have a defect or an issue? If not, why not?
- Does my root cause make sense?

Five Whys

Five whys is a problem-solving tool. Repeatedly asking "why" is a highly effective way to identify the root cause of problems. Asking why helps focus one's thinking while tracking the various paths to root causes. Asking "why" is the fundamental question of learning. Ask why until a root cause or several present themselves.

Pareto

Some team members may not be familiar with presenting data in a way that helps with analysis. One useful format is called Pareto. Pareto is a method for organizing data into groups from largest to smallest, highest to lowest, and so on. Conducting a Pareto analysis of the collected data is an effective way to identify the group with the greatest impact on a specific topic. The Salvarcar Transformation Committee used this tool to analyze and select transformation opportunities for the project teams.

Efficiency

Efficiency has long been a topic of discussion in organizations and will likely remain so. Efficiency tools can range from complex to straightforward. There are five fundamental steps to achieving efficiency, outlined below. Use these steps when improving efficiency is the goal. If an organization focuses on machinery rather than people, replace the human element in the five steps with a machine:

1. **People in the area are ready to work during scheduled work hours.** Be on time at the start of the shift, after breaks, and after lunch. Quit on time before breaks, at lunch, and at the end of shifts.
2. **People productively working during the time in the area.** Be at your assigned station performing assigned tasks, not walking around, talking with co-workers, or using the phone.
3. **Eliminate work stoppages—all time that prevents people from working while in the area.** Reset the area before each shift, including materials, work instructions, tooling, and other necessary items,

so it's ready for the next team. Workstations are equipped with materials, trained employees, online inspection, and online packaging, among other features. Record all factors that prevent people from working in the area and address those issues.

4. **Streamline and eliminate non-value-added work from the process.** Process map—ask the flowchart questions (listed in the flowcharting tool section). Eliminate delays, wasted motion, in-line work in process (WIP), non-value-added steps, and inspection where the process is in process capability index (Cpk) control. Combine operations and positions where possible. Balance the lines and workflow.
5. **Improve and automate the process.** Transition from manual to semiautomated, and from semiautomated to fully automated, where applicable. Automate—data entry, work instructions, inspection, and test. Simplify—work instructions: move to video work instructions (better aligns with the knowing, seeing, and feeling training model). The video instructions show how to perform the operation and the time required. Please note that it is critical to accomplish step 4—streamlining and eliminating non-value-added work from the process—before automating. There is a false economy in automating a process that has not yet been optimized. Optimize, then automate. There is value in optimizing a manual process before incurring the expense of automating it.

Cause and Effect Diagram

A cause-and-effect diagram (sometimes called a "fishbone diagram" due to its shape) is a popular way to analyze process issues by listing possible root causes under categories (the fishbones) such as manpower, machines, methods, and materials. These four categories are those most commonly used, but they can be added to or changed depending on the process being discussed. The problem forms the spine of the diagram, and the fishbones coming off the spine of the diagram help to focus a team on the different process segments that may cause or contribute to the problem being discussed. A cause-and-effect diagram is a type of brainstorming function and requires verification of root causes. If process experts are involved in the diagram development, the possible root causes are more accurate.

Flowcharting

Flowcharting is widely used. Wherever there is a system or a process, it can be represented by a flowchart. There is significant power in using a system or a process flowchart. An old saying is, "a picture is worth a thousand words." That saying is certainly true when representing a system or subsystem in a process flowchart. Once a system or a process is mapped out in a flowchart, it becomes easier to analyze.

Generally, flowcharting begins at the macro-systems level, identifying all first-level subsystems, their inputs, meaningful measurements, and outputs. After targeting a subsystem for transformation, it can be decomposed into a process flowchart, along with selected measurements of essential inputs, process steps, and outputs to focus on during the transformation.

Innovation involves navigating through different layers of subsystems until reaching the level at which innovation can occur. A flowchart can also drill down to the same level and provide detailed information at each process step to annotate the targeted measurement for transformation, whether it's process time, cycle time, manpower, material, energy used, maintenance costs, distance traveled, or any other measurable detail.

Flowcharting is a key component of various tools, including process mapping, Lean, Single-Minute Exchange of Die (SMED), white-collar productivity, work procedures, computer programming, and other tools that describe or analyze flows.

Symbols

Flowcharting uses symbols to represent process components. Many types of symbols can be used. Each symbol represents a process step and summarizes the function occurring at that point. There is no limit to the kinds of symbols that can be used in a process flowchart. The key idea is that a symbol should depict something recognizable and essential to the process being presented and analyzed. People can create their own symbols if they wish. Different industries and disciplines may have their own standard symbols used within their fields. The five most common symbols are: a rectangle for inspection, an upside-down triangle for storage or inventory, a "D" for delay (idle time in a process), an arrow for transfer, and a circle for an operation. Any symbol can be used, but it's important to include a legend on the flowchart explaining what each symbol represents.

Analysis

The purpose of flowcharting is to collect data for various symbols throughout a process. These data will be used to analyze the process and identify potential process steps for innovation and improvement. The relevant data to collect should be determined before creating a flowchart. The required data may vary from study to study, depending on the study's purpose.

Asking a series of questions plays a significant role in the analysis process. Do not skip these questions; they are crucial to transforming a system or process. The questions prompt a thought process that leads to innovation and improvement of each process step in the flowchart. Ask these questions at each process step.

- **Purpose**—What is the purpose? Why is it necessary? What would happen if it weren't done? What other method could achieve the same results? Can it be eliminated?
- **Place**—Where is it performed? Why is it done there? Are there other locations where it could be done more effectively? Can it be combined with another operation or rearranged in the sequence of operations?
- **Sequence, Time**—When is it completed? Why is it done at that time? Could it be done in a different order or at a more cost-effective time? Can it be combined with another operation or rearranged in the process flow?
- **Person (or machine)**—Who does it? Why does this person do it? Who else could do it more efficiently? Can it be combined with another operation or rearranged in the process flow? Can it be automated?

- **Means**—How is it done? Why is it done that way? Are there any safer, more profitable ways to do it? Can it be simplified?
- **Materials**—Why are these materials or chemicals used? Can alternative materials or chemicals achieve the same results? Is it possible to reduce the amount of materials or chemicals used? Could changing the shape or design of the material or part make it more cost-effective?

Improved Process Design

Based on the information gathered in the process flow, summarize the various types of information collected throughout the entire process. This may include total time, total manpower, total energy, total delays, total inspection points, total storage or inventory points, and so on. This information serves as the baseline for comparing various improvement options.

The improved process should significantly reduce total cycle time and eliminate steps such as transportation, delays, storage, and even operations and inspections. Bottlenecks and all types of waste should be removed from the process. Let the team's imagination run wild within guidelines and see what process transformation is achievable. After designing a new process, develop a process map flowchart that illustrates its structure and the latest summary data showing the before-and-after conditions.

Implementation

Implement the new process. This might require forming an implementation team specifically for this purpose, under the leadership of the Transformation Council. Identify the necessary resources, create a charter, select the right people from all departments to execute it, and apply effective change management techniques to achieve your goals. Implementing new changes can be an exciting time, a disaster, or anything in between, depending on the approach taken. Change management is crucial for successful transformations, particularly in addressing the people dimension of change.

White-Collar Productivity Study

Leading an organizational transformation project for white-collar departments can be quite rewarding for those involved. The improvements from these efforts are typically gratified by those impacted, as their work lives become more productive and meaningful. These initiatives can significantly reduce or eliminate many frustrations and root causes of wasted time for white-collar employees. Use this tool when working on white-collar transformation projects.

White-collar productivity studies utilize flowcharting of activities, and the data collected includes the time and costs associated with each activity. Instead of focusing solely on the ongoing expenses related to activities, attention should also be placed on tracking time, equipment, floor space, personnel, and cycle time associated with each activity or task. It's fascinating to observe what happens when individuals begin to understand the actual expenses tied to an activity, a report, floor space, or any other white-collar output. Much of the new technology development targets helping reduce the costs of white-collar activities. Understanding which activities add value in a white-collar context may require careful consideration and time. Once identified, all non-value-added activities can be focused on for improvement, automation, or elimination. AI is a key tool to consider for automating repetitive white-collar tasks.

Gathering Task Charting Information and Analysis

There are various methods to collect the necessary information for a white-collar study. All methods require data to enable a competent analysis. To gather information, select a method that aligns with the project's size and scope. It is essential to remember that the goal of all information gathering and analysis is to present the team with a prioritized Pareto list of tasks to focus on, thereby achieving the most significant transformation for the effort as quickly as possible. Only the top Pareto activities should be selected for the analysis questions phase. A manual data collection process is a fast and efficient method for gathering the necessary information:

- Gather a department or key department members into a conference room.

- Ask the group to list daily, weekly, and monthly activities along with the estimated time taken to accomplish each activity.
- List the equipment and other resources used for the activities. At a high level, include the building floor space, utilities, and other associated overhead costs.
- Estimate the importance of the outputs for the activities, in their opinion.
- List the roadblocks, obstacles, delays, and so on that keep them from accomplishing their activities and the associated time with each roadblock.
- For the top three Pareto activities, time-wise and expense-wise, do the following:
  - Answer the flowcharting analysis questions for each activity, including this additional question: "What is needed to remove the roadblocks, delays, and obstacles that hinder completion of the activity?"

The gathered information and the answers to the analysis questions will then be used to innovate, redesign, eliminate, combine, and modify activities. Do not skip asking the critical step of asking the flowchart analysis questions! Lastly, the redesigned activities will be implemented using a proper change process.

Single-Minute Exchange of Die

Shigeo Shingo was a Japanese industrial engineer renowned for his expertise in production systems, efficiency, and continuous improvement. One of his notable achievements was the development of SMED, which enhances the efficiency of setups and changeovers. This tool can be applied to low-volume, high-mix assembly lines, machine changeovers, scheduled maintenance, pit stops, or any similar processes where critical resources are temporarily taken offline until the changeover is complete. There are six steps to SMED: Observe and document the current process, separate internal from external activities, convert internal to external setup, streamline the remaining steps, implement the changes, and maintain continuous improvement.

Use SMED when focusing on a process changeover for a machine, assembly line, or other operation to reduce downtime caused by the changeover or setup. It employs flowcharting and process mapping during the analysis and innovation stages.

Additional Tools

Additional tools can be added to the transformation team's toolbox. Include tools that are meaningful to the organization and use them when the situation warrants.

Chapter Summary

- Improvement teams need basic training in project team management and in tools that can be useful for effecting transformation.
- Teams should receive team management training during their first team meeting.
- Training on basic tools can occur as the team advances in its assigned transformation project.
- Every company should have a toolbox filled with basic tools that can be shared and form a company wide knowledge base.
- Some basic tools for the toolbox may include: brainstorming, expert interviews, problem-solving, five whys, Pareto, efficiency improvement, flowcharting/process mapping, cause-effect diagrams, white-collar productivity, SMED, and other tools.

CHAPTER 6

Team Findings, Root Causes, Solutions

We now return to the three Salvarcar project teams, which were organized to initiate the transformation process. The teams employed various tools from the discussed toolbox; they held at least one team meeting each week, and the Transformation Council members appointed as champions for each team met with the team leaders to provide guidance and training as the teams progressed. The team leaders reported to the Transformation Council every two weeks on their teams' progress.

Identify the tools project teams use during the data-gathering and analysis phase as they begin to fuel their EOT. Consider the additional tools and analyses you would have used to address the issues the teams identified.

To accelerate the transformation process and train the Transformation Council, the council leader attended team meetings, assisted in training team members, and engaged in data gathering and analysis. This involvement facilitated the teams' progress without requiring them to wait for training at the council and team levels to commence. It also enabled the quick identification and implementation of "low-hanging fruit" and "just do it" opportunities. The council and team members navigated the learning cycle of Knowing, Seeing, and Feeling daily with someone who had previously led major transformation projects. All levels of the organization experienced a sense of importance, concern, and care due to the council leader's direct daily involvement and follow-ups, walk-arounds, training, and attention.

Resisting the False Tyranny of Speed

Every organization has a change rate capability, the ability to effect change. The change rate is not static and can improve over time through learning and experience. Part of the leader's responsibility is to recognize the current change rate capability and to ensure that the rate is not exceeded during the transformation process. Concurrently, the leader should strive to enhance the organization's change rate capability over time.

The change rate capability is similar to a performance curve and includes many performance components. Four of the major components are:

- **Desire**—There is no performance without a desire to perform. The magnitude of desire determines one's willingness to learn, practice, and progress. The greater the internal desire, the less external motivation is needed to enhance this performance component.
- Many organizations employ motivational innovations to help boost desire levels. This may include bonuses, promotions, attention, prestige among peers, or other strategies. Everyone has their desires and motivational triggers. One motivational innovation does not work for everyone. This should be kept in mind, and discussions with individuals may help clarify the motivation, if any, needed to achieve the right level of desire for success.
- **Mental and physical preparedness**—Training, practice, and experience fall into this component. The greater the training, developed skills, and experience, the greater the performance, provided the desire and innate capability are present.
- **Innate capability**—Some might say this is the God-given talent one is blessed with. Training, experience, and desire can sometimes compensate for a lack of innate talent. We have all seen situations where people with a strong desire can achieve performance levels that exceed those with more naturally gifted talent. However, if all other performance components are equal, the person with the greatest God-given talent will perform at a higher level than their peers. Care should be taken to focus on all major performance components, rather than prioritizing innate ability.
- **Stress or anxiety**—Some stress is beneficial and helps motivate one to move forward. However, excessive stress can impair both mental and physical capabilities, ultimately reducing performance. Greater knowledge and experience increase the amplitude of the performance curve and reduce perceived stress.

The goal is to identify the sweet spot on the multidimensional performance curve and operate there to maximize performance. The focus is on increasing performance, so work the equation to achieve this: increase desire, mental and physical preparedness, and keep stress within a healthy motivational range. Develop strategic plans and actions centered on the components of the performance curve to accelerate performance improvement. Continually optimizing each performance component will automatically increase overall performance output.

Every individual has their own performance curve. Each person's curve must be understood. The performance curve for an activity is linked to the performance curves of the individuals involved. This is not merely the sum or average of individuals, as group dynamics should be synergistic, yielding results that far exceed the sum of individual abilities.

Over time, improvement rates will increase, and change will become a regular part of daily activities, which, in turn, will lower the organization's stress levels—all of which are critical to facilitating organizational transformation.

Back at the plant, the three teams began their projects, drawing on the knowledge gained from prior experience and training. They analyzed the sublevel systems and processes, identifying actionable activities.

Material Variance Team

This team sought and obtained information on two key questions: Why was the scrap rate 14 percent, and why did material variance account for 20.3 percent of all annual expenses? Remember that scrap is a subset of material variance and was included in the 20.3 percent. The team conducted the following activities:

- They read three months of scrap tickets and categorized the information by defect code, quantity scrapped, person doing the inspection, and operators who created the scrap.
- They examined who was conducting the quality inspections, their training level and experience, and the location and timing of those inspections.
- They analyzed the time between when a glove exited the knitting machine and when inspection was conducted.

- They made a Pareto of the defect types and the employees creating the defects.
- They examined the experience, training, and seniority of employees who made defects compared to those who did not.
- For the defect codes, they researched root causes.

Here are the conclusions based on the analysis and the information gathered.

- The knitting operator position was being used as an entry-level position for new employees and was experiencing constant turnover.
- To receive increased pay, knitting operators could transfer to inspection, material handling, or any other position within the company. Knitting was one of the lowest-paid positions.
- Knitting operators did not inspect their gloves for all defect types emerging from the machines. They were deemed unqualified to inspect their work due to insufficient experience in identifying defects and adjusting machines to eliminate root causes. If an issue occurred, they were instructed to shut the machine off and call maintenance to address it.
- At each knitting machine, a large bin was placed to catch the gloves as they exited the machine. When a bin was filled with gloves, it was moved to the end of the work cell and replaced with an empty bin. Bins from all machines were accumulated and periodically moved to the inspection area. Each bin contained 40 to 50 pairs of gloves, which required three to four hours of machine time to produce. Remember that each machine produced one pair every six minutes.
- There was no in-process inspection.
- The bins of gloves waited in the inspection area for three or more hours before being inspected.
- When defects were discovered, the bins were moved to a rework area for correction, usually with little or no communication back to the operator who had produced the defects.
- Knitting machines have approximately 50 to 120 knitting needles in them, depending on the knitting bed size. Needles wear out at different rates and must be replaced. The knitting machines do

not know when a needle breaks or wears out, so they continue to run. An operator must identify the issue and stop the machine. Operators run 11 machines each and may not be aware of the problem for an extended period.

- Scrap was being entered into the ERP system by the part number found at the finished bill of materials (BOM) level. This overstates scrap costs, as each part number at each level above raw material also includes burdened labor. The burdened labor costs were already captured in the actual direct labor worked, so was being reported in the financial reports twice.

Solutions seemed so evident when the analysis was presented that it was difficult for the members of the Transformation Council not to provide immediate direction to the team on the actions to take. Remember, there is a transformation process to follow. Have faith in the process; it will work. "Be quick, but don't hurry," as Coach Wooden would say.[8] We need to stay in the sweet spot of the organization's performance curve while working to improve it. Helping teams learn and follow the transformation process will yield sustained results over time. Be patient and encouraging to the teams.

The leadership task is to ensure the future state is innovative, thereby maximizing performance within existing constraints. Transformation occurs in three phases: short-term, mid-term, and long-term opportunities. Select the opportunity improvements judiciously, based on a mix of implementation times and values. Help the teams understand that consistently improving financial performance month over month requires working on short-, mid-, and long-term projects simultaneously.

Efficiency Team

The Efficiency Team considered their question, "Why is efficiency so low, only 45 percent?" To better understand this question, they performed the following summarized activities:

- They worked to determine how long the machines operated during a shift, as the machines decide the hours earned for calculating efficiency, determined by the glove output. To achieve this, they decided to conduct random-time observations, using a random number generator to select times throughout the day to walk around and count the machines running on each line.

- They then spoke with operators to better understand the root causes for the machines not running.
- They provided logs for each machine so operators could note the reasons for the stoppages and the duration of each machine's idleness. Maintenance personnel recorded their actions to restore the machine's functionality, along with the time taken to complete the task.

Their significant observations and root causes were as follows:

- The machines were turned off when employees left for breakfast, breaks, and lunch. All employees left the area simultaneously.
- Many machines were stopped due to a lack of scheduling and configuration. Some machines ran only small gloves, some medium, some large, and some extra-large. There was some crossover between sizes.
- Operators lacked the training and experience to solve quality issues, adjust machines, load programming, and perform minor maintenance on their equipment, and had to wait for help.
- Machines stopped when a yarn spool emptied.
- Stopped for broken or damaged needles
- Stopped for programming for the next job order
- Stopped for minor maintenance and adjustments
- Stopped for major maintenance
- Stopped waiting for a maintenance person to have time to fix a machine
- Operators ran 11 machines each but were unable to keep all of them running due to the above issues.

This summary list was sufficient. Most items included additional details, which will become clear as the innovative future-stage solutions are developed and explained.

Cycle Time Reduction Team

The Cycle Time Reduction team considered the question, "Why does it take three weeks to process an average customer order?" To better understand this question, they decided to undertake the following summarized activities:

- They developed a process mapping flowchart to track material from the warehouse, through the production cycle, back to the warehouse, and until an order was shipped out to the customer.
- They analyzed history for customer orders to gather cycle time data.
- Interviews were conducted with the planners to understand the process of scheduling the manufacturing floor and the theory behind the method.
- They spoke with customer service to understand the customer order patterns.
- They collected ordering information and patterns from purchasing, along with the minimum and maximum order quantities from the ERP system for raw materials and finished goods.

The observations and root causes identified for the three-week cycle time were:

- Two planners independently scheduled different halves of the process. One was for the knitting operation, and the other for the overedge and palm-printing operations.
- The knitting orders were produced and sent to the warehouse for storage until the second planner scheduled the overedge and palm printing orders for production.
- The planners did not coordinate customer orders for build sequencing. The overedge and palm printing operations were scheduled based on customer need dates, but the knitting function was not always aligned with them. Sometimes it was, but not consistently. The knitting schedule estimate relied on historical data and a safety stock level for knitted glove liners.

- Each knitting machine had a large bin that gathered four to five hours of product before moving the material to the end of the work cell for temporary, in-process storage.
- Gloves were moved to the inspection area only after a customer order was complete. The order was kept together in one move to prevent bins from being lost.
- Gloves were not scheduled with a consistent lead-time aligned with customer needs. Some orders were scheduled weeks late to meet customer needs, while others were produced weeks in advance of the scheduled delivery date.
- Gloves were lost in the warehouse or on the production floor due to the large amount of work in process (WIP) kept between knitting, overedge, and palm print. This loss of gloves required that total or partial orders be reproduced before a customer's order could be shipped.

An interesting note: As the team investigated why gloves were missing from finished goods and WIP, and why orders had to be remanufactured, discussions unfolded during lunch among several team members and other employees. They discussed the details the team was addressing because non-team employees were curious about their co-workers' activities. One team member discussed the missing materials from finished goods and WIP, noting they were trying to determine how the gloves had gone missing.

The following Monday, a non-team employee arrived at work and told her friend, a team member, that she had discussed some team details with her cousin, who had come to visit. The cousin inquired about the gloves and how they looked. After receiving a description of the gloves, she mentioned that she had seen gloves matching that description for sale at the local flea market every weekend. The employee and her cousin then went to the local flea market and purchased some gloves. The employee brought the gloves to work on Monday, and, sure enough, they were among the missing glove styles being written off as scrap and material variance. This information was communicated to the Material Variance team and the Transformation Council.

This team provided valuable information on potential root causes. It became evident to both the team and the Transformation Council that there was significantly more room for improvement than anticipated. Still, we now understood one of the troubling root causes. A quick, positive major transformation was on the horizon.

It is remarkable how much information emerges when teams are genuinely focused on improvement and transformation. I wonder if the information would have been shared so readily if the council leader, the on-site executive, had not been engaging with the people on the floor and with different teams almost every day, taking an interest in what the teams were working on and their thoughts. People can tell when management is authentic, interested, and truly believes in the process being discussed.

Chapter Summary

- Resist the false tyranny of speed.
- Performance has several components that can be summarized under four headings: desire, mental and physical preparedness, innate capability, and stress or anxiety.
- Each of the four key performance components should be focused on for improvement.
- Every individual has their performance components.
- Training and experience can help to improve some of the performance components.
- Motivational innovations can be used to help improve desire.
- Every individual has their motivational trigger; learn what each needs and address it.

CHAPTER 7

Team Solutions and Implementations

In this chapter, we focus on the innovations, implementation actions, tools, and process control steps used by the project teams. The project teams' Engines of Transformation (EOTs) are fueled with analyzed data and are powering up.

Many operational issues require transformation, whether large or small. They are caused either directly or indirectly by the organization (consciously or unconsciously). Regardless of the reason for the transformation, the organization can find solutions. Often, all that is necessary is cross-pollination from individuals who have been through the "fire," so to speak, and have developed the skill of leading transformation, which they can then train others in, following the "know, see, feel" model of personnel development.

Over time, the transformation system becomes an integral part of daily business operations. People will adopt this mindset in their professional lives. One of the goals should be to foster an organization capable of independent learning and proactive action. When applied, the principles outlined in this book will achieve just that.

Early in the transformation process, it became clear that a vital resource was not assigned to the facility. An engineering R&D center was located 1,550 miles away in South Carolina. The center had six people managing glove designs and BOMs, and they were responsible for approving any specification changes. Being near Clemson University allowed them to partner with yarn manufacturers and those developing new yarn materials and technologies. One can understand why the VP of R&D placed that small group there; however, was it the best location for the company's benefit?

The R&D group was not very responsive to collaborating with the Salvarcar facility in Cd. Juarez, Mexico. Given the distance and reporting to a different VP than the operations facilities, it was all too easy to decline requests from the facilities to participate in the necessary transformations. There was no willingness to be involved.

After discussions at the executive level, the decision was made to relocate the North America glove R&D groups to Cd. Juarez. This facilitated greater participation in plant transformations and improved R&D by making manufacturing processes and staff available to design new products and processes. These products could be made using existing production equipment, or new methods could be developed to incorporate emerging technologies. It made sense for R&D to be co-located, allowing both groups to work together more effectively.

A change in the reporting structure was made so that R&D reported to the head of Western Hemisphere Manufacturing on a dotted line for factory support and to the VP of R&D on a solid line for the R&D portion of their work. Both executives provided input on the R&D employee evaluations.

During the first two months, it also became clear that some plant staff members were not in the correct positions, and some chose not to participate in the necessary changes. Those who needed to be replaced were, and those in the wrong positions were moved to where they could excel more in their profession and contribute to the necessary transformations.

The most experienced and capable engineer served as production manager, overseeing the production floor. Following a private, collaborative discussion with this skilled engineer, it became clear that he was not being used effectively. A joint decision was made to appoint him as the manager overseeing engineering, technology, and maintenance, and as the facilitator of the Transformation Council. He would manage operating procedures, technical training, equipment modifications, and the agendas for the team updates to the Transformation Council. He was responsible for coordinating engineering and technology efforts, both internal and external to the facility. Initially reluctant to make the change, he dedicated his heart, mind, and effort to the task and achieved great success. Eventually, he became a global expert, helping train other manufacturing knitting sites on the improvements and machine modifications implemented.

Next, the production department was placed under the quality manager's leadership. Some may ask, "How can production and quality report to the same manager? Is that not a conflict of interest?" Not when the right people, the right training, the right attitude, the right process controls, and the right culture are in place. When all the right "rights" are in place, it can happen and be successful. This turned out to be the case in Salvarcar.

Those who design the process, operate machines, and assemble the product are the ones who control quality. Quality cannot be inspected into a product; it is built in through effective process control procedures. Who better to lead production and the quality engineering group than someone who understands process capability and effective process control and is comfortable working on the floor with all personnel involved? In such a scenario, there is no finger-pointing and no turf wars. One person was now responsible for producing all quality products. Now that the necessary resources were available and properly positioned to make and implement all product and process decisions, the teams could move much more quickly through the transformation process.

As the teams began developing solutions to the list of root causes, they discovered that many key solutions could only be implemented through cooperation among all teams. The solutions generated had a positive impact across all teams and would also improve each team's metrics. This was intriguing but not fully understood at the outset when the team charters were created. Each department in the company influenced the performance of every other department. This fact strongly supports the need for cross-functional teams when creating charters and selecting team members. The redundant results and solutions developed by multiple teams will be presented only once to avoid redundant information.

Another notable outcome of the innovative solution development process was that two teams sought to form subteams to implement specific root-cause solutions that required development and experimentation. The teams requested that the subteams report directly to them, enabling coordination of activities and expedited solution implementation. Furthermore, as teams began implementing solutions, more employees offered ideas and expressed interest in joining teams to improve the processes they were involved in. At that point, the pace of change increased significantly, along with the excitement in the plant. The KPI metrics also began to trend positively and gained momentum.

Most of the presented implementations occurred over a three-year period as the teams progressed with their projects and formed subteams. Additional teams were added as more employees became trained and wanted to participate. Selected works of all these teams are presented together.

Cycle Time Reduction Team

After identifying the root causes and observations, the Cycle Time Reduction team envisioned the ideal outcome for the knitting operation. The charter they received indicated a reduction in the average cycle time from three weeks to three days. However, after reviewing data showing a knitting machine can produce one pair of gloves every six minutes, the team concluded the goal should be to fulfill an average glove order within 24 hours of issuing the job to the floor, rather than the original three-day target. This was their vision for the future state of the system. Although it seemed ambitious at first, they were committed to innovating and designing the process needed to turn that dream into reality. The most helpful tool for this team was process mapping, which involved analyzing each operation using the flowcharting analysis questions. Much of the implementation of cycle time reduction fell into the category of "low-hanging fruit," items that could be implemented quickly.

Innovations

The following item numbers correspond to the root cause items listed in Chapter 6.

Glove theft, items 7 and 8—The first action was for the team to seek assistance from the Transformation Council to address glove theft in the warehouse and WIP. The Council determined that the council leader and HR manager would interview all warehouse and material handler employees, explain the situation regarding the material loss and the findings at the local flea market, and inquire if they had any information related to this matter. It was believed that involving the site executive, who also spoke Spanish, in the employee interviews would lend significant weight to the situation and provide adequate cover for employees with information to share about the internal theft ring.

Something extraordinary happens when upper management discusses the transformations and then physically participates in the projects. This demonstrates commitment and signifies the importance of the changes being made. Additionally, it aligns with the management of change principle, which states that individuals prefer to hear about change and plans directly from top executives whenever possible.

As planned, the HR manager and council leader interviewed all warehouse and material handling employees. Three interesting things happened immediately: first, some employees were aware of the theft ring and provided names, having been previously afraid to do so. Second, the two warehouse personnel personally involved in the theft ring (the supervisor and one employee) left work while the interviews were ongoing and never returned. Third, there were no more missing gloves from the warehouse after that day. A side benefit of this effort was that not only was cycle time reduced, but material variance was also reduced, which helped another team reach its goal.

Glove planning and scheduling, items 1, 2, 3, and 6—The team reviewed the flow process map associated with material movement from when the knitting jobs were released to the floor until shipments were made to customers. Flowchart analysis questions were asked, and the following innovations were developed, transforming planning and scheduling.

- Bills of materials (BOMs) were all updated to a single-level structure, with all raw materials assigned to the finished goods part number level. This update enabled all raw materials required for a customer order to be retrieved from the warehouse simultaneously under a single job order and sent to the floor, eliminating the need for two additional job pulls per order and significantly reducing material movement to and from the warehouse. All raw materials and subassemblies were processed together through the manufacturing process until finished goods were produced and returned to the warehouse as ready-to-ship products. This action enabled a planner to schedule and track a customer's order through the entire manufacturing process by issuing a single job order.

- Customers were divided so that one planner could schedule jobs for half of the customers, while the second planner scheduled the jobs for the other half. Each planner oversaw the jobs from the moment the customer's order was received until the order was shipped and received by the customer. This arrangement ensured each planner always knew the status of every order, significantly reducing the time required to respond to internal and external inquiries about order status. This change eliminated the need to issue materials to the floor and then return them to the warehouse for each BOM level, along with the related ERP transactions and inspection paperwork. The manpower previously required for these extra movements, data entry, and inspection reports could be reassigned.
- All lead-times were applied at the finished goods part number level. This ensured consistency among similar glove styles and better managed the WIP on the floor, reducing the time jobs spend idle. Additionally, it eliminated warehouse storage time caused by a lack of lead-time coordination.

Glove collection bins and movement to the inspection area, items 4 and 5—The team assessed the sizing of the collection bins at each machine and determined a more efficient size. They also investigated the reasoning behind storing all finished gloves in the knitting area before moving them to the inspection area.

At this point, it quickly became clear that the Cycle Time Reduction, Efficiency, and Material Variance teams needed to collaborate closely to succeed. Just as the Cycle Time Reduction team helped the Material Variance teams by solving the theft issue, the Efficiency and Material Variance teams would also support each other to succeed and, in the process, help the Cycle Time Reduction team to overachieve their dream of the future state system and implement their remaining ideas:

- Small collection bins at the knitting machines that could only hold six pairs of gloves.

- Inspect all gloves in-line to remove the necessity of moving an entire customer order of product to an inspection area. Gloves are to be inspected, at most, in six-pair batches when removed from the machine collection bins. All inspections should be completed by the time the last glove on a customer order exits the knitting machine. This would also prevent the need to load the gloves into large bins and then unload them for inspection.
- The inter-team collaboration proposed to move the overedge sewing process to the end of each production line. This change was intended to eliminate the need to load gloves into large bins, then move them to the overedge area, unload them for processing, load them into bins after processing, and then move the bins to the warehouse to await packing into shipping boxes. The change would have the gloves process pass through an overedge knitting assembly line, where the gloves would be loaded into labeled shipping boxes and stacked on shipping pallets. When a pallet was filled, it would be sent to the shipping area to await completion of the customer order, then be loaded into the shipping container.

All glove styles, except those requiring screen printing, were included in the new process flow. The screen-printed gloves, which accounted for less than 10 percent of production, needed an extra processing step that couldn't be integrated in-line. However, these gloves could still be loaded into labeled shipping boxes, tagged with a colorful process label, before being moved to the screen-printing area. As a result, large storage bins and the related loading and unloading steps were eliminated from the process. All workers involved in non-value-added loading, unloading, and bin transfers were freed and moved to perform value-added operations.

After implementing the items mentioned above, the cycle time was reduced from three weeks (15 days) to just three days. The team was very enthusiastic as the transformation occurred on the floor and was eager to continue collaborating with the other two teams to achieve their ultimate goal of reducing the average cycle time to 24 hours, from the release of a job order to shipping finished goods to the customer. The team eventually achieved and surpassed that goal, shipping the average released order in just three hours.

After several weeks of running with the overedge sewing machines in-line with the knitting machines, team members asked if it was possible to knit the overedge into the glove while on the knitting machine, thus eliminating the sewing operation. After many weeks of research and development, engineering was able to design a wrapped elastic thread that successfully permitted the knitting of the overedge. Machine modifications were made to add that subsystem to the knitting machines and this new propitiatory process was successfully introduced.

Material Variance

The team charter directed the team to reduce the combined scrap and material variance from 14 percent to 5.0 percent, which was considered a reasonable initial target. The tools employed by the team included Pareto for prioritizing defect types, flowcharting for information entry, and pinpointing where process inspections and defects occurred. The team's ideal final system state was a process that wouldn't require external inspection. One where all defects could be identified and corrected immediately, thereby reducing the number of defects. They also had an additional goal of achieving 99.7 percent accuracy in warehouse cycle counting.

Material Variance Innovation and Implementations

Once again, the item numbers correspond to the root causes represented in Chapter 6. Innovated solutions generated by the team were:

Items 4 and 6—Were addressed by the Cycle Time Reduction team and were previously discussed. Smaller containers were implemented, and inspections were conducted in-line.

Items 8 and 10—Item 10 was not previously listed but was developed by the team as they analyzed glove defect data. The top defects causing scrap of knitted gloves were holes in the glove's finger, palm, or cuff; holes in the finger crotch; and holes in the fingertip. Additionally, there were mis-sized gloves that were too short, too long, or too narrow. To mitigate these defect types, the team addressed the following:

Holes in Glove Fingers, Palms, and Cuffs

The primary cause of these holes is a faulty needle latch that prevents the needle hook from grasping the yarn when the needle is actuated. The latch remains closed, so the yarn is not captured during knitting, resulting in a hole from a missed stitch. With each traverse of the knitting slide (which actuates the needles), the same malfunctioning needle fails to knit. This creates a progressively larger hole, row by row, until the defect is detected; the machine stops, and the needle is replaced.

By effectively using problem-solving questions and asking "whys," the team identified subsystem-level root causes. Why did some latches stop working on certain needles and not others? Where in the needle bed were the failures occurring, and why are the damaged needles not found in other locations?

Needles in the center of the bed are used more frequently than those on the outer edges. The central needles knit the middle three fingers, the palm, and the cuff of a glove, while the outside needles knit the thumb and little finger. The needles at the extreme edges of the bed only knit the tips of the thumb and little finger. Depending on the glove size being knitted, several needles may remain unused for specific sizes.

Why does increased usage cause the needle latches to fail? It makes sense that they would fail, but why? There are two reasons. First, as yarn passes through the needle hook, fiber fragments and yarn dust accumulate in the latch mechanism, preventing the latch from opening properly. Second, the latch mechanism wears out over time due to friction at the latch pivot points (metal wear), leading to failure.

The team arrived at a lower subsystem level where action and innovation could occur:

- Determined how often the needles needed to be blown off with pressurized air to remove free-floating yarn dust and fibers from the latches, using the central needles as the time trigger for cycles before cleaning. First, they verified the effectiveness of the cleaning operation using manual air hoses. Then, they followed the efficiency steps and modified the equipment to automatically eject pressurized air based on the number of completed knitting cycles.

- Determined the mean time to mechanical failure of the latches due to wear and then scheduled needle replacements based on that predicted time, instead of waiting for random needle failures to occur.
- Changed needles in various sections of the needle bed according to the frequency of use for the glove sizes being produced.
- To reduce maintenance costs and offline needle cleaning time, an inspection process was established to salvage, recycle, and reuse needles that were below a certain wear life. The wear time was determined by experimentation. Only new needles were used in the central sections of the knitting machines, while recycled needles were used in the outer sections, where usage was lower.
- The efficiency team also determined the downtime required to replace the needles on the floor, which was substantial when needles were replaced only on random failures. If all needles were replaced at once, it took 30 to 40 minutes to complete the swap, depending on the size of the needle bed. The team decided to purchase extra needle beds and load them with new and recycled needles. Then, when it was time to replace needles, they brought the replacement needle bed to the floor and completed the changeout in approximately five minutes. They no longer replaced needles section by section; instead, they replaced the entire needle bed based on a projected usage-to-failure cycle. They minimized needle-bed machine downtime by applying SMED techniques.

New Specification for Permitting Holes in Glove Liners

The changes mentioned above successfully reduced holes in gloves by approximately 85 percent, addressing the root cause of malfunctioning needles. However, holes were still being found due to other root causes.

During a team meeting, one of the members made an observation.

Over 75 percent of the gloves knitted are for liners, which are sent to Bermudez, where a foam nitrile dip occurs to coat the

> fingers, palm, and cuff on one side of the liner. Small holes will be covered, and once covered, the holes cannot grow in size. Small holes should be permissible in liner knitting.
>
> Someone else added to the conversation,
>
> A knitted glove is, by design, filled with holes. The space between each stitch is a hole. Machines can be programmed to create more or less space between stitches by adjusting the stitch tension. So, what is the difference between a loose stitch and a small hole? In a glove, a hole will begin to unravel over time, but in a liner, the hole cannot unravel once the yarn is captured in the foam coating.

These comments sparked significant discussion. Previously, all gloves and liners with a single hole, regardless of size, were discarded. In the spirit of effective process control, step one (clear specification) raised many questions that needed answers. Can you detect a hole in the liner once it is covered in nitrile? What size hole would be acceptable? How many holes in a single liner would be permitted? Where in the glove could a hole be acceptable? Design engineering had no data on this topic; no testing had ever been conducted in this area. Therefore, they agreed to perform some testing and return with answers.

After experimentation, the following comments and specification changes were made.

Comments:

- It is impossible for a hand to feel a small hole in the liner once coated with foamed nitrile. All spaces between stitches and holes are filled.
- Yarn cannot unravel once coated. However, they can unravel before coating due to liner handling.
- It is difficult for small holes to be found during in-line inspection in the knitting area. They are easily found in Bermudez when liners are stretched over the metal formers before coating. Final hole inspection should only be performed in Bermudez for liners.
- Most of the liner scrap for holes has been found in Bermudez. It is not reported back to the Salvarcar plant as scrap, so it has not been included in any of the information analyzed by the Material

Variance team. Consequently, scrap has been underestimated at Salvarcar. Improving the hole-scrap issue will reduce the scrap rate at Bermudez.

- Holes in the fingertips and finger crotches have a different root cause and cannot be permitted.
- The coating does not keep a finger crotch hole from unraveling because it is not entirely coated with foam. The fingertip holes may unravel over time with use, regardless of whether they are covered with foam or not.

Specification Changes:

- The palm can have one ½ cm hole or two ¼ cm holes measured when stretched during mounting on a metal former in Bermudez.
- A finger can have one ¼ cm hole when mounted.
- The cuff can have one ¼ cm hole when mounted.

Holes in the Tips of Fingers and Finger Crotches

These holes lack good stitches on either side of the hole. The fingertips and crotches mark the start of the knitting process, as the knitting machine is programmed to create a secure stitch at those points. If the stitch is missed, the glove will unravel during use. What causes the stitch to be missed? The first stitch is formed when the loose end of the yarn is grabbed and pulled under the stitch. This is achieved by directing a puff of air at the loose yarn end to blow it into place. Sometimes, the puff of air fails to direct the yarn correctly, preventing it from being held in position long enough to be properly stitched. The second stitch will be satisfactory, but the first will be flawed and will eventually unravel.

Innovative solution to this issue:
After experimentation, the following equipment innovations were made, which eliminated 95 percent of this defect type:

- Modify the air nozzle by flattening the end to create a wider fan of air injection, covering a larger area.

- Increase the air pressure of the injection to create a greater force, thereby moving the yarn faster.
- Increase the time of the air injection by a factor of 3.
- Increase the length of yarn on the free end to better assure capture for the first stitch.

Item 11—This item was also generated by the material variance and Efficiency teams and handed over to a maintenance subteam, which targeted to reduce costs for replacement parts by 30 percent. The team ultimately cut costs by 60 percent. Here is how they handled the needles, which was a very innovative approach that later became common in the industry. Other major equipment modifications will be included among the Efficiency Team's innovations.

- Knitting needle replacement for hook wear—The hooks wear out and break due to abrasion caused by the yarn rubbing against them during the stitching process. The team decided to coat the hook area with titanium, a more rigid material than the steel used for the needles. They found a shop in El Paso, TX, that could plate the titanium. Although the cost of needles increased by 30 percent, their lifespan grew by at least three times—a significant savings.
- Following the same thought process, other heavy-wear machine parts surfaces were plated with titanium and exhibited a 2× wear life improvement.

Item 9—The procedure for scrap data entry was changed from reporting data at a subassembly part number, including burdened labor and material costs, to breaking down the scrap by raw material and reporting it at that level. This eliminated the double reporting of labor expense.

Items 1, 2, 3, 5, 7, and item 3 from the Efficiency Team—These items address a significant issue affecting both quality and efficiency. The machine operators lacked the necessary skills to produce a consistently high-quality product. They were unable to adjust and set up the knitting machines, meet quality requirements, or take necessary action when defects were found. Moreover, each operator was responsible for running 11 machines. What could be done to solve this situation?

In the spirit of using the Why-Why tool, the key question was, "Why has the company chosen to have entry-level people run the knitting machines?" No one could answer that question. It appears that this approach has been employed for a considerable amount of time. The practice was that once an operator became proficient at running a machine, they were promoted to become an inspector, allowing them to identify defects made by new operators and help resolve those issues. Afterwards, they would transition from inspection to a material handler or a maintenance position, which were higher paygrade positions. The highest-paid hourly workers were in the warehouse and among the top few elite members of the maintenance crew, who were responsible for tearing down and rebuilding equipment. This approach was not logical, but it was the plant's current operating method, and it needed to change to move forward.

To tackle this core issue, a comprehensive overhaul of the hourly structure and compensation program was necessary. This issue needed to be escalated to a team that included members of the site Transformation Council for resolution. A new team was organized, led by the Council's leader, who had the authority to implement and approve any necessary changes. Also on the team were the manager of technology and maintenance, the production and quality manager, the HR manager, and two long-tenured supervisors who had spent many years with the company and were familiar with the details of most of the facility's operations and equipment.

The new team's goals included creating a training and progression matrix designed to decrease hourly pay levels from 72 to 25 or less. This would involve placing new employees in noncritical positions where they can assist without compromising quality. The purpose was to channel the most experienced individuals into critical positions where they could attain the highest pay, specifically in roles related to running and maintaining the knitting machines. This initiative was considered one of the most important, innovative, and transformational components of this vital turnaround project. The topic will be explored in greater detail once the Efficiency Improvement team's findings are reported.

Voice of the Customer

The Material Variance team held a brainstorming session to explore alternative ways to improve quality, unrelated to scrap and material variance. Since this did not pertain directly to the goal at hand, the comments were placed in a "parking lot" during the session. After the immediate facility shutdown threat was averted and the team had some extra time, they revisited the "parking lot" items. They delved into this topic, which revealed significant market growth opportunities for the company. The simple comment was,

> Let's get the voice of the customer, regarding their thoughts on the quality of our industrial gloves. We can ask them what they would like to see improved in the products they purchase from us, as well as what other products they wish were available that are currently not offered.

The sales and marketing teams were contacted to collaborate with the group and engage customers in gathering responses to the parking lot questions. The feedback from customers was valuable and interesting:

- For the current nitrile foamed gloves, the flexibility is great. Employees can pick up small parts with the current gloves, and the grip is excellent when handling dry components. Hand protection is adequate for non-cut-resistant applications.
- Workers experience hand fatigue due to the prolonged use of gloves. The fatigue points are with the middle knuckles of each finger after hours of opening and closing the hand. The entire hand gets fatigued fighting the tight knuckle points—it requires effort to close the hand into a fist.
- They expressed the need for a similar glove to the current style that would have a high cut resistance property for handling sharp components.
- A glove is needed with better gripping properties for handling oily and wet components, without losing the ability to pick up small parts from a tabletop.

- Customers stated they would be willing to pay a premium for gloves that could solve the above issues, because their workers' efficiency and health would be improved.

  Upon receiving customer feedback, the manufacturing and R&D teams collaborated to develop the following gloves to meet customer needs.
- The knit stitch spacing was increased around the middle knuckle on each finger so that the glove's profile matched the natural in-and-out shape of the fingers, where the knuckles have a wider diameter than the straight bone sections. The knit tension programming and increased knuckle spacing were patentable features that enabled the world's most comfortable industrial glove of this type. This new patent was issued, replacing the old expiring glove patents, and was immediately included in all knit and dipped glove types. As a result, these gloves, which remained the world standard, could be sold at a premium because of the comfort they provided to workers. The patents would protect the new designs for the ensuing 25 years.
- A new glove was developed and introduced to the market that retained the dexterity of the nitrile foam glove while incorporating a high-cut resistant yarn and a new nitrile foam-based dip coating that provided a firm grip when handling oily components. This glove commanded a higher price than the original comfort-improved glove.
- A new glove was specifically designed for handling water-based, wet, and slippery objects. The design required the development of a unique process that created pits of a specific size in the nitrile foam dip covering, which became a protected secret process. The glove exceeded market performance expectations and was well received.

The team's efforts not only saved the plant from shutdown but also resulted in the production of patented, market-leading industrial gloves that generated larger margins than other styles. The introduction of new products increased demand at the plant, leading to growth and higher production volumes. It is incredible how simple steps can lead to transformational products in the marketplace.

Chapter Summary

- Over time, solving problems, embracing transformation, fostering innovation, and committing to proactive improvement become integral to daily business operations.
- Everyone benefits when managers and executives spend time with front-line workers and perform their jobs. Understanding and trust develop among all involved.
- Transformation teams working on different projects can benefit from collaborating to help each other accomplish their objectives and goals.
- Co-locating all job functions related to a product line can enhance the speed and quality of product development, manufacturing, innovation, and quality.
- Assigning the right person to the right role is crucial for success at every level of an organization.
- Effective training programs are essential for operational success, requiring both classroom instruction and on-the-floor training. Remember the three components of performance improvement: Knowing, Seeing, Feeling.
- Listening to the voice of the customer can lead to innovative and improved products, as well as a larger market share.

CHAPTER 8

Efficiency Team Results

Nearly all types of efficiency follow a standard formula that applies to any person, organization, machine, or other item. This formula remains constant, with only the variables changing depending on the subject under study. It involves dividing the actual results of an activity by its expected results. Sometimes, the expected results are referred to as a "standard." Common examples of efficiency include: labor efficiency—the time it takes to complete an activity divided by the standard time; miles per gallon (MPG) efficiency—the actual MPG achieved divided by the published MPG the vehicle is expected to reach; and other types like machine efficiency, utility efficiency, and cost efficiency, all calculated using the same concept. It is essential to determine the most appropriate measure of efficiency for the specific operation under evaluation. Efficiencies for organizations and operations can and should be established, reported, reviewed, and corrective actions taken when warranted.

When developing an efficiency metric, it is essential to ensure that the scope is sufficiently broad to include all relevant data. Collecting only partial data when measuring efficiency is counterproductive and can lead to misleading results. A comprehensive efficiency measure provides a metric that cannot be easily manipulated or misrepresented, as it encompasses all necessary data.

The main point is that improving efficiency for the most critical inputs to a system or a process is crucial and should be monitored and continually refined. Critical inputs for efficiency measurement may vary between processes, depending on the specific inputs involved.

To better understand efficiency improvements, it is helpful to use the baseline standard when calculating efficiency as transformations are implemented. This allows for a clear understanding and effective communication of the advancements being made. Such a practice can also result in efficiency measurements exceeding 100 percent as new methods, procedures, and training take hold within the organization. Additionally, it provides a consistent metric for measuring progress that can be integrated into a bonus or reward system based on improvement. Some organizations may wish to use two efficiency measures: one for tracking improvements relative to a baseline, as explained above, and a second for assessing current efficiency levels based on the updated standards as process changes are implemented.

Efficiency Improvement Team Improvements and Innovations

While working on the facility turnaround project, the Salvarcar Transformation Council identified the need to measure critical inputs to their processes that had not been previously tracked, and they established standards based on current actual results. Then, they began analyzing the components and systems associated with each input, as discussed in the EOT model. This led to innovation and significant improvements. The results of their efficiency improvement efforts are now detailed.

The efficiency team considered the significant causes of inefficiencies presented in Chapter 6 and implemented the following innovations:

Item 1 and part of 10—Machines were turned off for breaks and lunch. This was low-hanging fruit. Personnel were asked to stagger their break and lunch times so that two of the three operators in each cell would always be available. Additionally, personnel were assigned to serve as floating operators, with one assigned to each two work cells. These floating operators helped fill gaps during breaks and lunch periods, as well as at other times of the day when extra assistance was needed to manage changeovers or other issues that arose. Some may ask, "Didn't this increase costs, when the goal is to reduce costs?"

The goal is to enhance efficiency, which requires improvement in all three efficiency metrics: labor, financial, and machine. As the financial efficiency vector improves, financial reports accurately reflect this progress, providing a credible indication of reality. In this scenario, the machines are the critical component of the efficiency and financial vectors because they are responsible for knitting gloves, which generate revenue. Keeping the machines running and consistently producing high-quality products is crucial. This highlights the importance of understanding the different values of each input to the process. If additional personnel are needed in the near term to keep the machines running, they should be added. This will promote a habit of maintaining the machines in good working order. As previously mentioned, workers were freed up by the actions implemented by all transformation teams. These individuals could be trained and utilized without increasing the facility's total cost.

Item 2—Due to the lack of available downtime information for the team to determine machine efficiency, a random number generator was employed to select times for walk-arounds during each day shift. The walk-arounds counted the number of machines running and those that were idle. This activity was conducted over five consecutive days, with 12 walk-arounds scheduled each day. The results were quite interesting.

- Considering all machines on the floor, the average percentage of machines running at any given time was only 15 percent. After reviewing two days of data, it was found that the two main reasons for downtime were machines being offline for lunch and breaks (addressed in item 1 above) and machines not being scheduled to operate.
- By removing downtime for lunches and breaks, as well as machines not scheduled to run, the runtime increased to 45 percent.
- The other significant causes of downtime were found to be those listed under the other significant causes of inefficiency items, and will be discussed in more detail under their headings.
- For the remaining three days of the study, additional categories were created to capture the machine sizes that were not operational and the general reasons for the downtime. The unscheduled machines included the small and extra-large glove sizes (5, 6, 11, 12+). Knitting machines were sold according to needle-bed size. Smaller glove sizes (5 and 6) were operated on one type of machine, sizes (7, 8, 9, 10) on another, sizes (10, 11, 12) on a different machine, and sizes (13, 14) on yet another machine.

The industrial workforce had the greatest demand for sizes 7 to 10; however, to meet the industry's requirements, sufficient machine types were required to cover all sizes. As a result, the larger and smaller needle bed size machines had more idle time.

The downtime caused by lunches and breaks was easily fixable and was already discussed in item 1 above. The idle nonscheduled machines, which also contributed to idle capital expense, posed a more complex issue that required careful analysis. A summary of the discussion follows. Observe how effectively some of the problem-solving and innovation steps were utilized.

- Why are four different models of machines needed to knit the four distinct groupings of glove sizes?
- It seemed reasonable that the larger needle bed machines should be able to knit any size glove from size 12 on down to size 5.
- Why is this not the case?
- Can you imagine the capital money, floor space, spare parts inventory, and downtime that could be saved if the large machines could knit all sizes?

The team became very excited about this and went to the floor to collect one of each of the four machine models, then took them to the maintenance room for further investigation. Word got out about what was happening, and several engineers and maintenance personnel volunteered to come in early or stay late, on their own time, to disassemble the machines and inspect the subsystem-level components for differences. Little did the team know they were instinctively following an innovation process: decomposing systems into lower-level systems and making innovative changes to those components, then rebuilding the system from the bottom up. What the team found out was:

- There was a shaft in each of the machines with holes drilled in it. The holes were used to insert a control pin that limited the knitting bar travel distance across the needle bed, thereby determining the different glove sizes.
- By drilling additional holes in the control shaft of the largest machine, all sizes of gloves could be made from a single larger needle bed machine. Wow!

- Creating smaller gloves on a larger bed size would result in some inefficiency because the knitting machine would still need to cycle from one side of the needle bed to the other before changing direction to knit the next row. This contradiction required resolution.
- The solution to reduce cycle time involved speeding up the knitting bar movement when it was not actively knitting, allowing it to move faster to the end of the needle bed and back to the next knit point. This increased speed was implemented across all machines once it was confirmed that the knit bar could move faster without compromising quality or causing damage.
- Some other minor changes needed to be made to machine components to make all of this happen.

The team was now prepared to conduct experiments on a modified large-needle-bed machine. As imagined, the smaller gloves were produced without issues, and after several days of experimentation, the appropriate knitting and non-knitting travel-time speeds were established.

An inventory of machine sizes versus demand was made, which led to the following conclusions and process changes:

- No more small needle bed machines would be purchased.
- Medium-sized needle bed machines would be modified to knit smaller sizes.
- Large needle bed machines would also be modified to produce medium needle bed size gloves.
- Based on this scenario, no medium-sized needle bed machines would need to be purchased for many years; just large needle bed machines would be bought.
- There was enough unused capacity in the current large needle bed machines to cover projected growth for the next one to two years.

As it turned out, demand exceeded expectations due to new glove designs released to the market, which offered improved cut resistance, oil grip, and water grip. New machines continued to be purchased after the excess capacity was consumed.

Much of the issue with machines not being scheduled was resolved through proprietary design changes that expanded the glove sizes produced on the larger machines.

Item 3—Lack of training: The training system was analyzed and found to be woefully inadequate. The training system was decomposed into subsystems, enabling innovation. This subject was partially addressed in the material variance section and will be discussed in greater detail in the Training and Progression matrix Team section. The pay structure was revised to reflect the second-highest hourly position: an operator running the knitting machines, inspecting their work, measuring against quality specifications, charting on SPC run charts, adjusting the machines, performing setups, and conducting minor maintenance. This was the job everyone aspired to, offering the highest pay, except for the senior maintenance roles, which had only four openings. The training required for the knitting machine operator position encompassed those of a junior maintenance mechanic, a quality inspector, and a machine operator. The details of how this was accomplished will be explained in Chapter 9. The knitting machine operators became so proficient that their product went directly from their lines to the Bermudez facility or other customers without further in-house inspection. The results of this position were that one operator could run 15 machines instead of 11. Glove production doubled with less manpower. The material variance rate decreased from 14 percent to 1.5 percent, and efficiency improved from 45 percent to 112 percent of the baseline standard.

Item 4—Machines stopped when the yarn spool ran out of yarn: The following changes were made to mitigate and mostly eliminate the root cause of stoppages:

- The nearly empty yarn spools were unraveled and then tied to a new full spool of yarn and rewound. This was accomplished while the machines were running.
- The purchasing department contacted the yarn manufacturers and arranged to purchase larger spools of yarn with double the amount of yarn per spool. This cut the number of empty spools that needed to be changed by half.
- Additional spool dowels were added to the machines to permit the storage of larger yarn spools to cover one shift of knitting, so

that operators did not have to walk to the central aisle to retrieve additional spools during their shift.

Item 5—Was addressed under item 11 with the scrap reduction team.

Item 6—Machines down for changeover: The team's practice was to run all machines assigned to a customer order until the last glove was produced, at which point they were taken down simultaneously. The lines were then cleaned of any remaining knitted gloves and raw materials. Afterwards, the new work instructions were distributed to the lines, and materials were allocated accordingly. The electronic codes for the next order were also entered into the machines. Only one person was assigned to load the new codes into the machine controllers, and this individual moved from machine to machine, uploading the information from a laptop computer. The downtime was excessive, given that each operator managed 11 machines. The innovations implemented by the team were:

- All machines were modified to permit connection to an internal Internet, thus eliminating one person having to visit each machine to download new codes physically.
- The electronic codes were moved from storage on CDs locked in a controlled cabinet to a controlled electronic vault stored online, which permitted many machines to have the code automatically downloaded at the same time.
- The process was changed so that more than one order could be run on a line at one time. As orders were nearing completion, a new order would be started on the line. Only one machine was taken down at a time, per operator, and then changed over while the other machines continued to run.

Items 7, 8, and 9—Waiting for maintenance personnel to come and make adjustments, perform minor and major maintenance. The following innovations were developed to minimize downtime for these types of issues.

- A training room was established with enough space to accommodate six knitting machines, allowing for each machine to be disassembled piece by piece and reassembled. All knitting machine operators were required to attend classes and undergo hands-on training before being allowed to operate a production machine. The training given was:

- The proper way to set up a machine, from downloading a code for an order to installing all the different yarns and threads, producing a first article, and all the quality checks associated with it.
- Effective process control outlines creating an out-of-control action plan to follow if a process is no longer producing to specifications. A small, multipage booklet, measuring 3 in. by 5 in., was developed and published to address the most common quality issues encountered by knitting machines and the necessary adjustments to resolve each problem. Each quality issue was presented on its own page, with the most frequently encountered root cause listed first and the least common listed last. Every page included the most commonly used adjustments to address the quality issue. Additionally, each quality issue was accompanied by multiple potential adjustment solutions, with the most common listed first. All operators were instructed to follow the proven solutions in the order provided. If a quality issue remained unresolved after exhausting all listed solutions, the machine was turned off, and senior maintenance personnel were summoned. The booklet conveniently fit into the front pocket of the smocks worn by operators and served as a quick reference.
- Minor maintenance tasks were taught to each operator, enabling them to maintain their machines independently without needing to call senior maintenance personnel.
- The SPC measurement taken was glove length, because a change in stitch size, too tight or loose, showed up in the glove length.
- SPC measurements and control chart plotting were taught, along with the necessary adjustments as dimensions drifted throughout the day. Slight adjustments were required to account for variations between yarn spools and to compensate for wear on needles and tooling.

- Quality criteria and inspection techniques were taught in the same classroom setting. While students were on break or at lunch, machines were adjusted or components replaced to create quality issues. When the students returned, they had to troubleshoot the machines and determine the necessary adjustments to return them to specification. Through this type of practice, the operators learned how to recognize quality issues, determine their root causes, and make the necessary adjustments to produce a quality product. This training developed a proficiency in using the out-of-control action booklet.
- The school lasted for two weeks, and students had to successfully demonstrate mastery of the above training to graduate to the next level.
- If a student failed the training, they could attend for a second two weeks. If they were unable to pass after that period, they were returned to a non-knitting position and waited six months before applying for the next knitting operator opening.

- An extra knitting machine and needle bed were stored in the aisle against the wall for every two work cells. If an operator determined that a machine repair would exceed 30 minutes, they could swap out the machine requiring major repair for the machine in storage and quickly bring it online.
- The extra floating operators were no longer needed to cover lunch and breaks because three operators could manage the entire work cell during those periods. The machines ran continuously without stopping. The floating operators were primarily used to assist in running machines while a normal operator worked on minor machine repairs on the floor. They were also available to help during lunch and breaks, when not filling in for those repairing machines.

Item 10—Operators were unable to keep 11 machines operational due to the issues mentioned. The results of the school and training showed that, over time, operators were able to fine-tune their machines, resulting in a significant reduction in downtime, an efficiency improvement to 112 percent, and a decrease in material variance to 1.5 percent. Positions for all but four members of the maintenance department, most quality inspectors, and setup operators were eliminated. Those skilled surplus employees were retrained and became knitting operators. As previously discussed, the knitting operators now perform minor maintenance, setups, and quality functions and earn the highest hourly wages, except for the four senior maintenance workers.

Some might believe that the increased workload for the knitting operators would harm production by causing more downtime or diminishing their focus on machine operation and quality. However, this was not the case. Those in maintenance, quality, and operations became skilled and successful in their new positions as knitting machine operators. Those who lacked the necessary skills transitioned to roles as material handlers, clerks, and other lower-skilled positions. The efficiency and quality improvements, along with enhanced training, enabled each operator to run 15 machines while exerting less effort than when they operated 11 machines before the improvements were implemented.

Unanticipated Benefits

Some unexpected benefits arose from the innovative changes made to the knitting equipment. The knitting machine manufacturer observed that the timing and quantity of purchases for new equipment and spare parts had changed. The number of knitting machines purchased each year had decreased, and the types of machines now being ordered focus on larger needle-bed machines.

The vice president of marketing at the knitting machine supplier called me to ask why the purchasing pattern had changed. I briefly explained that we had modified the machinery, enabling us to knit gloves in all sizes on a single machine. Additionally, some machine components have been modified to increase production speed and extend the service life of needles and other heavy-wear components.

The VP did not believe that increasing machine speed could be achieved without sacrificing product quality. He insisted that their engineers had already maximized the equipment's operating speed, and he also doubted that a large machine could economically produce gloves of all sizes. I briefly summarized the results of the major design changes made as follows:

- Holes generated in the fingertips and finger crotches were now almost eliminated.
- The machines can vary speed in the same knitting row—moving fast when transversing the needle bed but not knitting, then slowing down to knit.
- High wear surfaces on needles and machine parts were being titanium-coated and oil-impregnated to extend wear life.
- The machine codes were now being remotely updated in mass at the same time via internal Internet connections.

No specific details regarding the changes were provided, nor were the maintenance modifications and training discussed. I assured the VP that the modified machines were now the most efficient and highest-quality glove knitting machines available anywhere in the world.

A couple of days later, the VP called me back and requested permission for two of his design engineers to visit the Salvarcar facility and review all the changes made to their equipment. The request was denied, with the explanation that the modifications were proprietary information to our company and provided us with a market advantage over the competition.

A week later, the VP called again and asked me to fly to Japan to meet the company president, tour the production facility, and visit local sites. They offered to cover the entire trip. I agreed to fly out to speak with them, but did not accept their offer to cover expenses. My company covered all my travel expenses to avoid any appearance of impropriety.

In Japan, the same discussions that had previously taken place over the phone were now held in person. Permission still had not been granted for their engineers to visit the Salvarcar facility. After a day's visit, when it was time to leave, the same discussion occurred once again. This time, I told them that if they provided a permanent 15 percent discount on all future equipment and spare parts purchases, two engineers could visit the plant and we would gladly show them all the design changes that had been made. The 15 percent discount was to be 15 percent lower than any price offered to any other global customer. The Marketing VP stated that they would need to discuss the suggested discount with the company president and would get back to me within two weeks. Two days later, upon my return to the Salvarcar facility, I found a message regarding the acceptance of the 15 percent permanent discount offer. The engineers visited for two weeks, and design disclosures were provided. The 15 percent discount proved sufficient to cover a significant portion of the salaries for the Salvarcar professional staff.

Chapter Summary

- Efficiency can be measured on almost any process input and output.
- Ensure that all critical process inputs are accurately measured.
- Not measuring critical inputs may lead to less optimal decisions.
- Make measurements more inclusive to avoid gaming and reduce measurement errors.
- Utilize the innovative process to break down systems into subsystems to effect change, and then rebuild the subsystems to a new and improved high-level state.
- Leverage transformations to gain a competitive advantage in the marketplace.

CHAPTER 9

Training and Progression Matrix

We often hear that "People are our most important asset." However, companies sometimes do not act as if they genuinely mean it. Employees are often expected to perform their duties without adequate training, tools, support, and an appropriate organizational structure. To maximize success, a company must have the minds, hearts, and energy of its employees.

At Salvarcar, one way this concept gained significant traction was by developing a training and progression matrix that made education, training, career paths, and salary advancement speed accessible to each individual. There were very few limitations in this program that were beyond each employee's control. The program included training, skill mastery demonstration, consistency, and teamwork.

The development of the matrix, its implementation, and the reception by the hourly workforce, along with the results achieved through this effort, will now be discussed. To simplify the discussion, let's refer to the training and progression matrix as the Matrix.

Why Was the Matrix Developed?

It was painfully demonstrated by the KPIs that the current operational structure of Salvarcar was not adequate for success. All KPIs were negative. Just by walking around the facility, one could tell that people were in the wrong positions, indicating a lack of training, poor performance, inadequate teamwork, and insufficient care. There was little pride in craftsmanship among the workforce, and 8 percent of employees were leaving every month!

How Was the Matrix Developed?

A Matrix transformation team was established with sufficient authority to make and implement decisions at all levels of the facility. The team included the head of Western Hemisphere Manufacturing, the HR manager, the operations and quality manager, the engineering and maintenance manager, and two longtime supervisors well versed in all areas. Additional individuals, including direct labor (DL) and indirect labor (IDL) employees, were invited to meetings to discuss the duties associated with specific positions and processes.

All current hourly positions, along with their corresponding pay grades, were listed on flip-chart paper and taped to the walls of a conference room. A summary of job duties and functions was generated for each position and added to the list. Similar job functions were grouped.

The team identified the purpose and outputs of the Salvarcar system. Its purpose was to produce high-quality industrial gloves at a competitive price. Its outputs include knitted glove liners for the Bermudez facility and finished industrial knitted gloves, shipped directly to distributors and customers.

The most critical job duties and functions in the hourly ranks that help meet the system's goals and outputs were identified. Most critical was defined as a position requiring extensive training to achieve proficiency. It's a role where a mistake can lead to significant product loss and equipment damage, for example, by comparing one person operating multiple machines to someone working on a single glove or unit at a time. Additionally, the time required to train and become proficient in the role was considered.

At this point, a lengthy discussion over several days compared positions and generated a list ranked from highest to lowest criticality. After reviewing all positions, comparing them, and discussing training time, the time required to achieve proficiency, and the potential damage to the product or equipment if an error were made, the team was ready to make decisions. These decisions would differ from what the staff had previously thought before putting in the effort to reach this point.

The team ranked the most critical positions from top to bottom. A shortened, summarized list of the innovative, newly created top five positions is listed in order:

- **Senior maintenance**—Could completely disassemble and rebuild machines, plus do all that a knitting operator, inspector, and maintenance person could do.
- **Knitting operator**—One who could operate and set up a machine, download new code to it, one who understood quality criteria and could make machine adjustments to eliminate defects, and learned basic SPC as well as how to measure and chart glove length data.
- **Inspectors**—This will transition to a more auditing role. Understanding quality criteria and how to measure and record data is essential. This position is considered to be at the same level as a warehouse worker.
- **Warehouse worker**—Moderate training and familiarity with raw materials, as well as data entry, are required. Candidates must understand how to enter data into the ERP system and perform accurate inventory counts. This position is considered to be at the same level as an inspector.
- **Material handler**—Not much training was involved, and almost no ability to make a grave error.

Pay bands were assigned to positions based on their level of criticality. This was a little tricky, and great care and judgment were needed. The following innovations were made:

- The number of positions at each level was determined. That number was closely monitored to prevent overpopulation at any level. The senior maintenance personnel were the highest-paid, and four held that job title. Each senior maintenance worker was assigned lower-level helpers to handle most of the less-skilled maintenance tasks. This allowed the senior maintenance group to focus its efforts on activities that required greater skill and experience.

- The remaining maintenance team was reclassified as knitting operators. Since they already knew how to adjust and operate the machines, they only needed additional training on the quality requirements. Fortunately, there were enough maintenance personnel available to ensure that at least one was present in each work cell. These experienced employees became leaders and core trainers for the other four operators in each work cell, teaching them the intricacies of machine maintenance and adjustments.
- Some inspectors were assigned solely to an audit role. The other quality inspectors already had training and experience with product specifications; they were later trained and moved into knitting operator roles. This transition was voluntary, but many employees chose to switch because the new pay rate exceeded their current inspector salaries.
- The best existing knitting operators were chosen for the new knitting operator roles. Each was paired with a trained inspector and a trained maintenance operator for on-the-job training until the training program was developed correctly and ready.

At this point, extensive discussions took place about how to implement all the transformations. These changes would impact every employee in the hourly workforce. Many employees were currently earning high hourly wages for positions that would be classified under significantly lower pay scales in the proposed Matrix. To maintain their current pay, they would need training and reassignment to positions that might be uncomfortable for them. All employee sentiment, both positive and negative, resulting from this transformation, would need to be evaluated, with plans made to address any issues that arise. Information must be prepared for each of the 1,100 employees affected by the restructuring. Four months were allocated to complete the movements once everything was in place and the time had arrived to start this major transformation. The change was expected to happen one work cell at a time. The social effects of this change remained uncertain. The implementation of the first two work cells would be used to determine the project's overall schedule.

Since all employees were assigned to future roles based on their current hourly pay rates and skills, consideration was given to each person's ability to learn and adapt, potential for skill development, and how each would respond to being placed in a new role. The goal was to ensure that no one would be laid off as a result of this restructuring and operational change. Based on these factors, employees were grouped by similarity, and customized communication was created for each group.

Each vertical pay band level was divided into four horizontal pay advancement quadrants. Employees moved through the quadrants based on the training they completed, the timing of their skill demonstrations, and their level of teamwork. Standard criteria were developed to facilitate advancement both vertically into higher pay bands and horizontally across quadrants.

These criteria included no unexcused absences, workplace accidents, or administrative actions in the previous six months. All quality, efficiency, and demonstration of living the company values requirements have been met in the past six months. Each employee was evaluated on teamwork by their supervisory team and work cell peers, including their willingness to collaborate, assist team members, share knowledge, and participate in training.

Training criteria were established for each quadrant within every pay band. The training was split into two segments: classroom instruction and hands-on practice with the knitting machines in the training room. Both parts required passing tests to evaluate knowledge and skill. Some training requirements for a knitting operator serve as examples of how training progressively builds across a pay band from one quadrant to the next:

- **Quadrant 1**—training on knitted glove quality and defect criteria, glove measurement and SPC charting, machine adjustments for out-of-specification issues, minor machine setup (changing yarn on equipment), and machine operation
- **Quadrant 2**—training on minor machine maintenance, meet efficiency and quality goals for quadrant 1
- **Quadrant 3**—advanced machine maintenance, meet efficiency and quality goals for quadrant 2, help provide floor on-the-job training for quadrant 1 and quadrant 2 employees
- **Quadrant 4**—advanced setup (includes downloading program codes and machine programming), meet efficiency and quality goals at quadrant 3, provide on-floor training for quadrant 3 employees

Example for the Knitting Operator Level M

Job Pay Level	Common Criteria	Q1 Criteria	Q2 Criteria	Q3 Criteria	Q4 Criteria	Next Job Pay Level
Knitting Operator Level M	**During the previous six months, NO:** Unexcused absences Workplace accidents Administrative actions Unexcused lates **Company Values (evaluated by supervisor and coworkers):** **Integrity** —in all things **Teamwork** —(assist team members, share knowledge, participate in training). **Stewardship** —(metric results **Innovation** —(participate to improve the knitting system **Ratings:** Acceptable or needs Improvement	**Training:** **Knitting** quality and defect criteria **Glove** measurement **SPC** charting **Machine** adjustments for out-of-specification **Minor** machine setups **Machine** operation	**Training:** **Minor** machine maintenance **Meet Q1 metric requirements for six months:** **Efficiency** 75.0% **Quality** 95.0%	**Training:** **Advanced** machine maintenance **Provide** floor training for Q1 and Q2 operators. **Meet Q2 metric requirements for six months:** **Efficiency** 85.0% **Quality** 97.5%	**Training:** **Advanced** machine setups (download codes and machine programs) **Provide** floor training for Q3 operators. **Meet Q3 metric requirements for six months:** **Efficiency** 95.0% **Quality** 99.0%	**Senior Maintenance Operator** **Level N**

Figure 9.1 Training and progression matrix

Figure 9.1 illustrates the information that each row in the Matrix should provide. There is one row for each position. Note that the last column in a row indicates the next advancement opportunity available to the employee, should they choose to pursue it and an opening exists.

An interesting note: In Salvarcar, training was held either before or after shifts, and employees completed it on their own time (without company pay). This might or might not work as well at other facilities. The pay increase for the knitting operator position was so significant that employees were willing to come in outside regular hours to train.

Training was completed, and certification was earned before promotion. Once training was finalized and certification obtained, employees waited for a vacancy to open so they could advance to the next vertical pay band. Training was required before transferring from one quadrant to another within the same pay band, and there was no limit on the number of employees allowed in any given quadrant of a pay band. Employees could take training in advance while waiting for the required time in their current position to pass.

Seniority for progression to a higher vertical pay band was based on the date on which all training and other requirements for entry into the first quadrant of the next vertical pay band were completed. Neither the length of time worked at the company nor the hire date affected the timing or availability of promotions. All promotions were performance-based.

It is important to note that if the need arose to increase the number of employees in a pay band, there were two options. First, employees who had been trained, certified, and completed their six-month tenure in the position would have priority. Second, if there were not enough trained, certified, and tenured employees available to fill the vacancies, then exceptions could be made to waive the tenure period and move employees immediately into the available positions once they were trained and certified. This required approval from the management and HR departments. No employee could be promoted to the next vertical pay band or quadrant without training and certification. This was a strict rule.

Implementing the Training and Progression Matrix

Designing a new training and progression matrix is one thing, but great care must be taken to implement it in a well-thought-out and well-planned manner. It is essential to reiterate the importance of utilizing change management to address the human aspect of change. Follow the process steps and ensure all necessary levels of communication are addressed. Even the best-designed employee programs can fail dramatically if not implemented correctly. Below is the process that was followed during the implementation of the new Matrix.

A general communication was presented to all employees by the head of Western Hemisphere Manufacturing that explained the following:

- **The need for change**—the factors driving the change: material variance, inefficiency, high turnover, and the current upside-down pay structure, among others.
- **Present relative data**—Some of the data developed was explained to present accurate information about the current financial state of the facility. While most employees were aware of some of these details, no one understood the full situation, and everyone was surprised by the operation's serious condition.
- **Present a summary of innovative solutions**—By this time, the transformation teams had been working for months, and the

teams had developed various innovative transformation plans. These individuals were peers of those in the audience, and all employees were aware that work was happening behind the scenes, with some updates being presented formally and informally during this period. There was significant interest in understanding the results of these teams and how they would affect each employee. Information was provided, emphasizing discussions on which operations were most critical to the company, the need to align pay with the time required for training, and the criticality of the operations being performed.

- **Present the new training and progression matrix**—A summary of the Matrix was given. Then the vertical pay bands, along with potential earnings by band, were provided. The criteria for advancement from quadrant to quadrant were discussed. Great emphasis was placed on the living company values criteria for advancement, followed by the training, certification, performance, and tenure-in-position criteria. A discussion was provided on the decision to give maintenance and inspection personnel the first opportunity to transition into knitting operator positions. All employees were notified that their employment would be retained and that no pay cuts would result from aligning the workforce with the Matrix.
- **Individual departmental meetings**—All employees were informed that additional information would be shared with each department later in the day, and questions concerning how each department would be affected and the opportunities available for individuals would be answered. Everyone had the chance to ask questions and get answers. About 75 percent of the employees became excited about the opportunity to advance and earn a higher salary. Approximately 18 percent were apprehensive about operating knitting machines, yet they wanted to earn that kind of money without actually operating them. It was reiterated that those who manage the knitting machines will earn higher wages. The decision was left to them. If they wanted the extra money, they needed to receive training and transition to knitting. No one was forced to move. Eventually, people understood the point. The

remaining 7 percent did not want any changes to their jobs and were uncertain about staying with the company. Most of that 7 percent decided to try the change, but made no promise to remain with the company. Fair enough, honesty is essential on both sides during these discussions.

- **Meet with Individuals**—Individual meetings were held between HR and each employee, with the employee's supervisor present, to discuss the employee's status regarding unexcused absences, accidents, administrative actions, quality, teamwork, and efficiency. Additionally, areas needing improvement and strategies to achieve those improvements to qualify for advancement on the Matrix were discussed.

The priority was to develop training materials. The Engineering and Senior Maintenance teams began setting up the training area and developing training resources. The quality department created inspection quality training for all levels.

The enormous scale of this workforce restructuring reminded me of a story Dieter F. Uchtdorf told in a November 2008 conference talk about moving a piano in a church in Darmstadt, Germany. A group of men was asked to move a grand piano from the chapel to the social hall for an activity. The men surrounded the piano and tried to lift it, but without success. Many people had ideas about where the men should be positioned to lift the piano most effectively, but still couldn't succeed. Finally, one said, "Brethren, stand close together and lift where you stand." Everyone stopped moving around to different positions, stood close together, and lifted where they stood. The piano rose off the ground and was moved to its new location. Uchtdorf concluded his story by saying, "That was the answer to the challenge. They merely needed to stand close together and lift where they stood."[9]

No significant transformation project is ever perfect. Sometimes, it's just time to move forward and "lift where you stand," making modifications along the way. That was the case with this transformation; training was not documented, and the training room was not prepared. No one had experienced a transformation like this, and as a result, they did not know what to expect along the way. The decision was made to proceed as best we could with what we had.

Current resources were assessed to better understand how they could be utilized to bridge the gap between our current system and the envisioned future system of a fully equipped training department with all necessary tools and training materials in place. Two essential groups of resources were crucial to bridging this gap.

First, experienced maintenance employees worked with the knitting work cells to maintain the existing equipment. This group was highly skilled and significantly underutilized. Second, experienced inspectors who understood all knitting defects and quality criteria reviewed gloves throughout the day as part of their role. If these two groups were given responsibility to teach and work in assigned cells, they could share their knowledge with the current knitting operators, who could, in turn, share their expertise and frustrations with them. This exchange could foster greater teamwork and provide the collaboration necessary to transform both culture and the manufacturing process.

The goal was to equip each knitting operator with skills in maintenance, knitting, and inspection. Therefore, a fully trained future operator must have knowledge of all three areas to function correctly. Perhaps they could teach each other so that everyone could eventually share the same skill and knowledge base. They might also be able to collaborate proactively, working together. This was the main idea, and the hope was to advance the transformation.

The maintenance department was structured with one maintenance person assigned to each work cell. These individuals quickly started providing on-the-floor training and operating machines. Additionally, one inspector was assigned to each work cell to conduct inspections and train all knitting operators on measurement, charting, and quality standards. No knitting operators were moved from the work cells. As a result, the staffing of each work cell increased from four operators to six. This manpower growth in work cells was achieved without increasing the overall plant headcount. Existing employees were reassigned to knitting work cells and encouraged to use their skills and to "lift where they stood."

As knitting operators trained and gained experience in minor machine maintenance, adjustments, quality inspection, measurement, and SPC charting, inspector personnel began to learn how to operate knitting machines. Maintenance staff began spending less time on training and on minor maintenance tasks, allowing them to focus more on troubleshooting problematic machines and optimizing their performance. With the temporary structure put in place, a few weeks later, the number of unplanned machine stoppages reduced, enabling the operators to manage 15 machines each, up from 11.

As training advanced and employees moved across the Matrix quadrants, efficiency improved, and three knitting operators became capable of operating 15 machines each. Consequently, headcount decreased from six operators down to three in each work cell. The surplus employees were absorbed to address early attrition from the transformation and to cover growth. Machine downtime had significantly dropped, as had scrap and material variance.

As humans, we are blessed with two good eyes. Keep one focused on the goal and the other on the process that leads to it. Daily, maintain consistency with manufacturing process controls and the organization's culture; the goal should be achieved automatically.

Following the EOT system is essential to reaching your goals. After all, processes are designed to meet the future imagined state system. Be sure to adjust the processes during the journey as improvements are identified, which may accelerate the achievement of the desired results.

Chapter Summary

- It is essential for companies to identify and tie every position in a facility to the criticality of achieving the desired company outputs.
- Ensure that pay band levels align with the company's criticality.
- List all training and results needed to qualify for advancing to each level.
- Develop and list the company's general requirements and values that must be met to be eligible for advancement.
- Measure and communicate the general requirements and training to each employee on a consistent schedule (e.g., monthly, quarterly).
- Control the number of employees that can be at a given vertical pay-band level and adjust it as business conditions change.
- Start the improvement process where you currently are. There is no need to wait until the training and organizational structure are perfected before beginning.

CHAPTER 10

Employee Evaluations

By the end of my first year as a young supervisor, it was time to evaluate all the employees who reported directly to me. This would be the first time I had the opportunity to evaluate staff. I felt both excited and nervous. I was excited because I was a young supervisor learning how to manage people. Still, I was also anxious because I had never evaluated anyone before, and most of my direct reports had significantly more seniority than I did. All of them were older than I was, with two of my direct reports being 40 years my senior.

My boss met with me to explain how annual evaluations would be conducted. He handed me the evaluation form, which was five pages long and included seven questions per page. Each question had a rating scale of 1 to 10 that I was to use to indicate the employee's performance. Each question also included a space for comments, where I was to list examples to support the ratings given. The instructions stated that I was to complete a form for each employee, have it approved by my manager, and then meet with each employee to review the form with them.

Now, I was really concerned. How was I supposed to rate my direct reports when each of them was older than I was? What was the difference between a rating of 6 and 7, or 7 and 8, or 3 and 4? What criteria were to be used for the scale of possible ratings? Nothing was mentioned or measured during the year for each of the 35 characteristics that needed evaluation. What was the purpose of the annual employee assessment? Merit increases were decided by the HR department and approved by my management. Was the evaluation part of that process?

I decided to do my best since people's future pay might depend on it. Writing as quickly as possible, each employee's evaluation took 75 to 90 minutes to complete. With 12 direct reports, I spent approximately 16 hours completing the evaluations.

I was proud of the work I did, completing all the evaluations quickly. I was excited to sit down with my boss to review each employee evaluation and hear his feedback. After my boss barely scanned the seven pages of the first evaluation, he said, "Wow, you wrote a lot of detail for each question. No one ever does this. I do not have time to read all the information included in your evaluations. What I do is quickly look at the ratings to see that everyone is not receiving the same ratings." As he spoke to me, he flipped through the pages, glancing at the ratings. After 10 minutes, he approved the 12 evaluations to be shared with each employee. I left my boss's office feeling let down that he showed little interest in the detailed information, let alone in understanding why I had written what I wrote.

Next, I met with my direct reports one-on-one. I made copies of the evaluation to give to each employee. Some employees showed interest in the detailed information. Most did not. Some asked why they were rated a six rather than a nine in a category. Some asked the meaning behind the 35 different questions.

One of the longtime employees sat down and looked at his copy for five seconds before standing up to leave. I asked where he was going and encouraged him to sit down to review the information for each of the 35 questions. He replied, "San, you are new to supervision. These evaluations mean nothing; they are a waste of time. The information written down is not used for anything. The ratings do not determine raises. The forms are to complete an HR requirement." I eventually convinced this employee to sit down and talk for a while, but we didn't discuss his evaluation. He wanted to share his history of assessments and explain why he had those feelings. It was very enlightening.

Sure enough, when raises were announced, they did not necessarily align with the evaluations; some did, and some did not. When I asked about this, my boss informed me that it was too complex to use the 35 questions to determine each employee's value to the company. Not all questions were relevant to evaluating an employee's importance. The boss created a totem pole of all employees based on his estimate of each employee's value to the company, and this was how raises were developed, approved, and distributed. I wish he had told me this in the beginning, and I could have saved many hours of tedious work generating all those evaluations.

Does this real story sound familiar? Over the years, the annual employee evaluation process has undergone significant changes. Some are complex, as in the example just explained, and some are simpler. Personally, I do not understand the need for an annual evaluation. Supervisors and managers should discuss projects, work assignments, and results with their employees frequently, or continuously as projects and day-to-day work advance.

I believe that a supervisor is responsible for training, mentoring, providing feedback, and helping each employee grow and improve. If an employee receives a poor evaluation, it should certainly reflect poorly on the immediate supervisor, with rare exceptions. The issue is that supervisors are seldom, if ever, held accountable for having employees with poor performance reviews. Generally, employees are held responsible for their poor reviews, but are they the root cause of poor performance? Some employees, particularly those who do not want to learn or perform, should be identified and removed from the workforce well before their annual review. Why wait and endure poor employee performance until review time?

Often, annual reviews categorize employees into quadrants based on their performance compared to peers with similar job titles. These rankings often influence salary adjustments, promotions, and workforce reductions. Most of the time, the rankings are based on management's opinion rather than hard data. Managers usually control the opportunities, training, feedback, and assignments provided to their employees. As a result, they wield considerable influence over who receives high-visibility assignments, enabling certain employees to stand out and make a positive impression on management. There must be a better and fairer way to assess employee performance!

Quotes from two prominent industry consultants and trainers whose careers have had a profound influence on the business world will be cited. Both of these esteemed mentors advocated for changes in the annual employee review process. They were W. Edward Deming, the renowned quality and operational guru, and Stephen R. Covey, the celebrated educator and author of *The 7 Habits of Highly Effective People*.

W. Edwards Deming

One of the things Deming was well known for was his desire to eliminate the annual employee business review and replace it with a more systematic, interactive process. He believed that annual employee evaluations did more harm to employee morale than good. Here are some Deming quotes on the subject. Look for the reasons behind his strong feelings and what he suggests would be an appropriate way to conduct employee assessments:

- **From his book, *Out of the Crisis*—Second Edition**[10]
  "One gets a good rating for fighting a fire. The result is visible; can be quantified. If you do it right the first time, you are invisible. You satisfied the requirements. That is your job. Mess it up, and correct it later, you become a hero." And, "Merit rating rewards people that do well in the system. It does not reward attempts to improve the system."
- **From *The Essential Deming: Leadership Principles from the Father of Quality***[11]
  "The merit rating nourishes short-term performance, annihilates long-term planning, builds fear, demolishes teamwork, [and] nourishes rivalry and politics. It leaves people bitter, crushed, bruised, battered, desolate, despondent, dejected, feeling inferior, some even depressed, unfit for work for weeks after receipt of rating, unable to comprehend why they are inferior. It is unfair, as it ascribes to the people in a group difference that may be caused totally by the system that they work in."
- **From Dr. Deming's introduction to the *Team Handbook***[12]
  "The fact is that the system that people work in and the interaction with people may account for 90 or 95 percent of performance. In such a situation, you then would have to measure most importantly the interaction with others and the system to evaluate someone."

To summarize Dr. Deming's views on evaluating people, an assessment should include three key components: an employee's interactions with others, their engagement with the system in which they work, and the improvements they suggest to enhance the system. This indicates that performance is influenced by three factors within the system that guide and shape efforts and interactions with colleagues. Does the employee correctly follow system processes to achieve expected results? Does the employee suggest innovations to improve system performance? Does the employee appropriately interact with others in the system? How are these three evaluation components taught, demonstrated, promoted, and assessed?

What is management's role in assessing an employee's interaction with the system and other staff? Care must be taken to ensure proper training, mentoring, and measurement of the "standards" for interacting with the system and colleagues. The system's performance cannot exceed its inherent capability. There should be a theoretical maximum performance for each system. Surpassing this maximum would require innovation and transformation to improve its capabilities. This should be measurable.

Stephen R. Covey

Covey also spoke out against traditional annual employee reviews. He favored replacing yearly employee reviews with creating "win-win," or employer–employee contracts that benefit both employees and the organization. He believed employees and managers universally dislike annual performance reviews. In August 2005, Covey wrote an article for the *Chief Talent Officer* magazine.[13] Two extracts of his article are:

- Referring to supervisors and managers, he states, "Instead of reviewing performance, they sit down with their employees and make 'win-win agreements.' The employee defines what the win is for him or her, and the leader defines what the win is for the organization."
- Referring to the contents of an employer–employee agreement, Covey says,

> First, you define together the goal of the agreement—the desired result. Then you define, again together, the guidelines, resources and accountability mechanisms you will use—that is, how and when you will account for progress on the goal. Finally, you define the wins for both of you if you achieve the goal—and the consequences if you don't.

Covey appears to suggest that employee evaluations should consider not only the company's expectations but also what matters to the employee. This information should be reviewed and analyzed in conjunction with established goals, metrics, and a reporting schedule. Moreover, there should be a clear outline of the consequences for both achieving and failing to achieve goals during the evaluation period. It is entirely reasonable for an employee's raise, bonus, promotion prospects, or other important factors to be tied to goal achievement in the employer–employee agreement.

Building on Covey's ideas, the manager would be responsible for providing resources (training, tools, funding, and so on) and helping remove roadblocks as they arise, so the employee is not hindered by the company while pursuing the agreed-upon goals. Managers should likely be assessed on their performance in fulfilling these responsibilities. Consideration might also be given to implementing consequences for management that fail to fulfill their commitment to provide resources and clear the path, thereby enabling employees to work toward achieving the agreed-upon goals. All of this will contribute to the integrity of the continuous evaluation program.

Remember that in Chapter 3, we covered the Transformation Council's responsibilities, including a two-week reporting cadence for discussing metrics and progress toward teams' goals. The team leader presents information, including requests for assistance, and reviews accomplishments from the past two weeks and plans for the upcoming two weeks. These biweekly reporting sessions also provide the Council with an opportunity to offer feedback, guidance, and support to the team, helping them stay on track to achieve their goals.

Implementing a similar approach to an employee evaluation program could significantly enhance, and even replace, the traditional annual evaluation process with a more continuous employee assessment program. Select an appropriate cadence to review the progress of the employer–employee contract.

Transforming the Employee Evaluation Process

Before transforming the annual employee evaluation process, it's helpful to ask questions that can define the necessary innovations.

- What is the purpose of the annual employee process? What is trying to be achieved? Answering these two questions will enable the development of a detailed system that leads to the desired results.

- Can the purpose of the annual employee review be achieved without conducting a 10- to 15-minute performance meeting with the employee once per year?
- Perhaps the annual meeting can be replaced with regular weekly, biweekly, or monthly meetings held between a supervisor and employee?
- Can those meetings be modified to include goal tracking, training tracking, results, and discussions about innovations that can enhance the current systems and processes, allowing the purposes of the annual review to be achieved without needing to meet for that actual review?

What typically happens during an annual employee review? We have all experienced those reviews at some point in our careers. Perhaps your experiences have been similar to mine? I will summarize the many annual reviews I have participated in. Those reviews have varied in duration from 5 to 15 minutes and have addressed part or all of the following topics:

- Here are some things you do well.
- Here are some things you can improve.
- Let's review the key metrics you are responsible for and see if the goals were met or not.
- What special projects did you work on this year?
- Is there some training you would like to receive this coming year?
- Here are your metric goals for the coming year.
- Here is your performance rating for this past year and your penetration into the pay range for your position. Based on that, your raise and bonus will be …
- Is there anything else you would like to talk about?

Should an employee be left in suspense for a year before being told what they do well and what they need to improve? Employee development should be a year-round topic of discussion, encompassing both the training the employee wants and the training the company requires. Supervisors should share responsibility for the employee's development. Who is the expert accountable for monitoring the employee and providing feedback on how to perform their assigned tasks? Indeed, supervisors should facilitate the development of those in their charge and provide regular feedback and support to enhance employees' performance.

Key metrics and goals should be reviewed and discussed daily, weekly, and monthly, depending on their nature. Both the employee and the supervisor must be aware of the status, and discussions should occur if the metrics and goals are not tracking as desired. Discussing last year's goals during an annual employee performance review seems redundant, since the conversation should be ongoing throughout the year.

Is it the employee's performance or the system's performance that determines the annual raise? As Deming stated, 90 to 95 percent of performance is determined by the system and interactions with other employees within the system. It would be helpful to receive immediate notifications about system issues so they can be resolved quickly, thereby reducing their impact on goal achievement. Management and other employees may need to take action throughout the year to give the employee being evaluated a fair chance to meet their assigned goals.

Annual raises could be more effective if they were not strictly annual but instead tied to a framework, such as a training and progression matrix that measures how well an employee embodies the company values, interacts with others in the system, completes training, and demonstrates the ability to perform at a higher level. Salary adjustments should be linked to specific milestones in the Matrix, triggered by meeting requirements rather than just the passage of time. Employees should be required to perform, grow, and contribute to the system to earn more than just a cost-of-living raise.

As we ask more questions and consider the reasons for conducting annual employee performance reviews, it becomes clearer that eliminating the yearly review could benefit both the company and its employees.

Create a Continuous Employee Performance System

Now it's time to innovate and transform the annual employee evaluation process, or, in the spirit of Deming and Covey, to eliminate it and replace it with a different type of process that can provide guiderails for performance and growth, and delineate the responsibilities of both the employer and the employee in achieving performance goals.

Let's take Deming, Covey, and the Transformation Committee system and put them in a bag. Shake the contents to mix the ingredients, and see what emerges. Perhaps it will be something new? Indeed, it will be an exciting and beneficial endeavor to support organizational and cultural transformation.

Following Deming, we evaluate an employee's interactions with the system, their interactions with other employees within the system, and their innovations to improve the system. This requires training employees in the "know, see, and feel" of interacting with the system and other employees within it, as well as understanding the expectations.

From Covey, we focus on creating a document that outlines what is important to both the company and the employee. Goals are developed around these agreed-upon priorities, with implications for meeting or not meeting them, affecting both the employee and the company based on each individual's performance.

Within the Transformation Committee system, we adopt a structured reporting cadence, incorporating goal metrics and periodic reviews to assess what was achieved during the previous period and to outline planned achievements for the upcoming defined period. Additionally, this provides an excellent opportunity to evaluate the performance of each side of an employer–employee type of document. Either party can request any necessary guidance, training, resources, or assistance, with feedback flowing in both directions.

Company Values and Culture

Most companies have published values that drive their culture. Some have three or four, while others may have ten to fifteen. To effectively integrate values into an employee performance system and foster culture, a company should have three to four values. Exceeding this number can complicate efforts to build a cohesive culture. Choose more inclusive high-level values that encompass sublevel values, permitting for the use of only three or four core values. If the organization operates internationally, choose terminology that translates effectively into the regional languages spoken by employees.

Do values follow culture, or does culture follow values? Many companies publish values, but their culture does not necessarily embody them. To transform a culture, follow the same Transformation Committee system used for any transformation, applying the EOT and all other items contained in the system. A culture system is simply the sum of the organization's current subsystems, their processes, and all the elements contained within. If a culture needs to change, that decision is based on analyzing data to understand the current state of the company's culture. The next step in the EOT is to innovate—imagine the company's future culture, then design a process to achieve it. Then, apply process controls to the designed process to ensure its success. Remember, it is the process that leads to reaching the goal. Examine the company's system and subsystems, focusing on those that require transformation to meet the envisioned cultural future state. Finally, reconstruct the transformed subsystems into the culture system you envision.

Values should be incorporated into other company documents to support cultural transformation. Job descriptions need to be revised to reflect the company's values and to illustrate how those values are lived in the context of the role. Continuous employee evaluations can be designed to include these same values. Suppose the employee evaluation is to assess the employee's interaction with their work system and with co-workers within the system, as well as suggested system changes that should be implemented. Such an employee evaluation process would naturally need to include the company's values and how exemplified.

What's Important to the Company?

Part of the evaluation process involves addressing key company priorities. Every company is unique, so the significant items may differ. Some fundamental topics will serve as examples and include:

- **Company values and culture**—four high-level values:
  Stewardship—the practice of responsible planning and management of resources for the benefit of the company and others. This could include being proactive, working through issues to accomplish daily work and goals, and coordinating with others outside the immediate team to "get stuff done."

Teamwork—work accomplished by a group acting together, where each member contributes to the overall efficiency. This may include assisting other employees within the work system, providing training, sharing ideas, or expressing gratitude to team members through an internal company social media platform, among other activities; however, a company wishes to define what teamwork entails.

Innovation—the ability to develop and implement new ideas, methods, processes, or devices that enhance the system you work with.

Integrity—honesty, true to your word, trustworthy, dependable. Integrity is listed last, but overarches and permeates all the other values and functions of the company.

- **Quality Requirements**—meeting quality expectations.
- **Performance expectations**—meet established and agreed-upon goals and objectives.
- **Employee professional growth**—additional training received and demonstrated in the job. Training can come from internal and external sources, including books, seminars, on-the-job training, and classroom instruction.

What Is Important to the Employee?

Employees have items that are important to them, just like the company does. Some of these important items should be captured and listed in an ongoing evaluation program. Many of the employees' significant items require the company to commit to and uphold those commitments to the employee. If a company culture is built on values, such as integrity, this should not be an issue. An employee evaluation program should be a win/win for both the company and the employee. Some topics that may be important to the employee include:

- **Personalize training**—implementing a personalized training program for employees to support their professional growth.
- **Provide resources**—Ensure the company commits to providing the resources needed to help meet expected goals and daily performance expectations.

- **Performance feedback**—receiving timely feedback on performance regarding important company matters.
- **Transformation teams**—securing opportunities to join transformation teams to improve the system they work in.
- **Connect pay to evaluation results**—creating a personalized, detailed program that connects pay raises, bonuses, and other incentives to evaluation metrics.
- **Share evaluation metrics**—distribute the evaluation metrics on a predetermined, agreed-upon cadence.

Designing an Evaluation Format

A company may use multiple evaluation formats to assess employee performance. A company with hourly employees may use a training and progression matrix to evaluate employees. Distribute employee metric data monthly. This informs employees of their standing relative to the requirements outlined in the Matrix. An evaluation format for salaried personnel would differ from the hourly format, but it would still cover similar topics.

Job Descriptions—Since evaluations are based on comparing performance to a standard, job descriptions should include the information needed to define that standard. List the four company values and provide a description of each. Additionally, the five to seven most essential functions for the job position should be outlined, with each function thoroughly described. The description should illustrate, through the five to seven job functions, how to embody each of the company's values in practice. The measurement methods used to evaluate compliance with these values can also be specified, ensuring that both the employer and the employee understand how performance will be assessed.

For convenience, all this information can be combined into a Matrix called the **job integrity matrix** (JIM). The JIM helps to embed the company's values at the heart of the organization by incorporating them into job descriptions and the evaluation process. Design a Matrix or other presentation style that suits your organization's needs. An example of the information needed to develop a JIM is provided below.

Example of a Job Integrity Matrix

The JIM outlines five to seven key job functions for a position, along with the metrics used to measure each function. It also explains how these functions align with the company's values. As an example, let's reference the **manager of product development** position, which includes the following five key job functions:

- **Supervise the customer service department**—involves interacting with customers to receive orders and address any questions they may have. Additionally, this role coordinates efforts with the sales force and the facility to which the orders are assigned.
- **Quote new business**—involves coordinating with the quoting engineers, purchasing, and advanced engineering teams to develop pricing for new customer products
- **Member of the global customer service committee**—involves participating in the committee, which meets quarterly to coordinate policies and procedures for all customer service functions. Its purpose is to enhance the efficiency of customer service operations and foster teamwork and synergy between locations. Additionally, to innovate and enhance the customer service functions and systems.
- **Develop annual customer pricing**—involves updating all company pricing annually and coordinating the annual contracts with customers
- **Develop and train customer service personnel**—involves developing tailored growth programs for each customer service representative and delivering departmental training to build a high-performing, cohesive team

Let's use the key job function of "quote new business" as an example to illustrate the type of information that would be included in a JIM for each key job function. The company value of integrity underpins all an employee's activities. Similarly, it encompasses the entire JIM and can be represented by adding it as a Matrix header row that spans the matrix. The Matrix row corresponding to the key job function example is shown in Figure 10.1.

Example for key function Quote New Business

Position: Manager of Product Development

Integrity					
Job Function	**Stewardship**	**Teamwork**	**Innovation**	**Resources**	**Measurements**
Quote New Business	Gather information from customers and internal sources to prepare quotes for new business. Ensure that quotes align with the company's margin requirements. Submit quotes to customers after completing internal review and approval.	Collaborate with purchasing, advanced engineering, design engineering, operations, finance, and customers.	Assist in developing systems and processes to shorten the time needed to generate quotes for new products and improve the accuracy of the financial results from those quotes.	Quoting and ERP systems, advanced engineering, operations, IT development, along with costing and standards databases, and additional personnel as needed.	New product introduction revenue generated over the last 36 months, time to quote report, error report, and financial reports for revenue and margins by customer.

Figure 10.1 Job integrity matrix

The JIM serves not only as the foundation for a job description but also as a framework for a continuous evaluation program. The JIM encompasses the critical components of an employee evaluation or employer–employee agreement, including the employee's interaction with the system, the people within the system, methods for improving the system, the resources to be provided, the individual's responsibilities, and the metrics used to measure results.

To create an employer–employee agreement, use the JIM and set goals for key metrics and list essential items from both the company and the employee. Any special projects to be completed should be listed, along with the expected consequences of meeting or missing the target goals.

Evaluation Review Cadence

Once an employer–employee agreement is created using a JIM and the other essential components, the final step in establishing a more ongoing employee evaluation process is to set a review cadence.

How often should a supervisor review an employee's performance on different aspects of a continuation evaluation process? The answer depends on which part of the employee assessment is being reviewed. Not every element of the employer–employee agreement needs to be evaluated at the same time. If an employee is working on a high-priority project, the supervisor might check in two or three times a week to monitor progress, address obstacles, and give feedback. If the task involves demonstrating the value of integrity, it probably happens daily as part of routine activities. For the teamwork value, a team survey would likely be conducted once or twice a year to collect feedback from team members. Other items on the evaluation Matrix may only need a review once a month or once a quarter. Set a suitable schedule for reviewing each item as part of the normal business process.

That said, it may be wise to schedule a more formal meeting with the employee to review all measurements and status at least every three or four months, ensuring that all items are discussed and allowing both sides of the evaluation process to provide feedback. Immediate conversations should also be held when new measurement reports are issued, especially if results are negative, to develop plans to address the situation.

Remember that the goal is to create a continuous evaluation process that replaces the annual review with a more effective teamwork dynamic between the supervisor and the employee. Items can be added to or removed from the employer–employee assessment agreement over time, keeping the document current and relevant as needed.

When it's time to provide a pay increase, the evaluation information is available and has been reviewed, so there are no surprises. Both sides of the evaluation process are aware of the predetermined raise amount, based on the performance outlined in the employer–employee agreement and the results produced during the evaluation period.

Chapter Summary

- A traditional annual employee performance evaluation program probably does more harm to employee morale than good.
- 90 percent to 95 percent of performance is determined by the system and employees' interactions with it.
- The annual employee evaluation program should be replaced with a more continuous evaluation process.
- An employee evaluation form should include:
  - Items deemed important to the company, including company values.
  - Items deemed important to the employee.

- How the employee is to interact with the system and with other employees in the system.
- Innovations the employee has submitted to enhance system performance.
- Expected results and how results will be measured.
- Responsibilities of the company to help the employee meet the goals.

- Linking company values to employee job descriptions and evaluations can help transform a company's culture; establishing a JIM is an effective way to make that connection.
- The cadence for reviewing various elements of an evaluation can vary depending on the need.
- There should be no surprises when raises are given out based on performance evaluations, as both parties involved in the evaluation process are aware of the standings at any given time.

CHAPTER 11

Bonus and Commission Programs

Bonus and commission programs are standard in industry. These programs can serve various purposes, but when implemented effectively, they can help change culture and boost productivity and innovation. The goal of these programs is to generate motivation and rewards that encourage performance toward reaching company goals. If mismanaged, the intended benefits may not be achieved, and it could lead to frustrated employees or other workplace issues. There are seven key points to help minimize problems for employees and the company while maximizing positive results: be self-funded, include everyone who drives results, offer enough value to motivate, avoid rewarding bad behavior, be measured in a way that can't be manipulated, have a time frame that matches the goal, and pay promptly after results are verified. Let's briefly review these seven points and how they relate to both bonus and commission programs.

Be Self-Funded

The bonus money comes from an increase in margin money. To clarify, let's define margin as revenue minus expenses. Keep in mind that the increase in margin money must be shown in the financial reports to be considered legitimate. The process changes implemented must generate a sufficient increase in margin money to cover employee bonuses or commissions, as well as enough to pay the company's portion of the increased margin. Without the company receiving its share of the funds generated through improvements, a bonus or commission program cannot be sustainable.

What should be the distribution of the increased margin money allocated to employees versus the company? That depends on the nature of the process. The more control employees have over the process output, the higher the percentage of the increase they should receive. A good rule of thumb is that the increase in margin money should be roughly 40 percent for employees and 60 percent for the company, especially in industries with high labor content where labor controls the pace and quality of output. There may be situations where employees receive a larger share of the split. It all depends on the process and specific circumstances.

When a process is automated and employees operate machines, with the machines mainly controlling the pace and quality of output, the division should tilt more toward the company, such as a distribution of 30 percent for employees and 70 percent for the company. Choose a division that fits your company and the process being improved.

Include Everyone Who Drives Results

Ensure that all employees involved with the system participate in the bonus opportunity based on their defined contribution, as outlined in their employer–employee agreement. There is little worse for a bonus program than excluding key participants, whose efforts are essential for the successful implementation of change. Here are a few examples:

Hourly efficiency improvements generate increased margin money. Implementing these improvements often requires input and effort from engineering, supervision, and other support staff. Everyone involved in developing and implementing the improvements should be rewarded to some extent for their contributions. The distribution of rewards doesn't need to be equal among all groups across the various disciplines involved. Hourly staff may receive a higher bonus rate than support staff if they are the ones exerting the most significant effort to enhance efficiency and productivity. However, all should be recognized for their level of involvement. Teamwork is essential for maximizing success.

A process that increases margin money through automation, installs new technology, drives innovation, and transforms the process should employ a different bonus distribution formula than the first example. The company is investing capital to enhance operations as designed by the employees (engineers, designers, and so on). In this type of improvement, engineers, designers, and the company may be entitled to a higher percentage of the increased margin as a bonus. Hourly workers should also benefit from the bonus because they operate and maintain the equipment. Thus, the bonus should be allocated to various types of employees based on their contribution to the improvement. Every employee involved in the process is crucial to success, and everyone's voice must be heard and valued for progress to be made. Teamwork and synergy will ultimately prevail.

Sales and marketing personnel acquire new customers and increase the company's margin by driving higher volume and, consequently, revenue. Who are the individuals truly involved in generating new business? Sales and marketing teams engage with customers. Engineering designs the latest products and interacts with customer engineers. New processes are developed and implemented. Work documentation and BOMs are created. Customer service ensures that customers remain informed and satisfied. Purchasing negotiates favorable pricing for materials, which helps win bids and enhance margins. The key point is that everyone involved in acquiring new customers and products should be part of the same commission or bonus plan. Each participant can receive a different percentage of the bonus payout based on their effort and involvement in the process; however, everyone must be included to maximize success and increase the margin money. Teamwork, synergy, and innovation are essential in achieving positive results.

Offer Enough Value to Motivate

The question becomes how much bonus to pay? Many studies have examined this question. The answer is not straightforward because everyone has different needs and desires; therefore, rewarding a general population with a monetary bonus program requires careful consideration and customization. Not all pay band levels should receive the same percentage of bonus opportunity. Generally, the threshold for a financial bonus to be considered motivational is 10 percent. Keep that in mind when designing a bonus program.

A bonus may consist of several elements that collectively contribute to a total percentage of opportunity. For example, the bonus element may include more than one goal: increased margin (covering most areas of improvement), on-time delivery of a key project, or another significant metric. The key is to have the entire bonus be self-funded. Some bonus goals may not be self-funded, but they should be tied to a self-funded goal whose achievement is necessary to receive a bonus payout. An employee should have the opportunity to earn a bonus based on their performance across all or some of these elements. Additionally, they should have the opportunity to exceed the bonus percentage by exceeding the target. Exceeding a goal generates more margin money than anticipated, so share the extra with those who created it. A program that incorporates this type of component is motivational.

As bonus potentials are determined for all pay levels, generally, the percentage of opportunity increases the higher one moves up the pay scale. The reasons are numerous, given the span of control and responsibility required to drive transformation across a larger revenue base. In previous chapters, it was emphasized that senior leadership should be deeply involved in Transformation Councils and lead the change effort. If they achieve favorable financial results, they should be rewarded.

Avoid Rewarding Bad Behavior

Care should be taken when selecting KPI measures to include in the bonus program. Occasionally, the KPI is poorly chosen, rewarding individuals for undesirable behavior. Here are two examples of this issue.

Example 1—The sales and marketing team receives a bonus based on increased revenue. They earn a percentage of the extra revenue generated. Bonuses were paid quarterly according to orders received. Some members of the sales team focused on maximizing their earnings by pursuing low-margin businesses and those with low volume and a high mix of products. The product mix differed from what the company was accustomed to managing.

Results—These actions consumed resources and overhead in ways that were not accounted for or measured in the bonus plan. The high mix required significant indirect labor to support changeovers, purchasing, and warehousing. Additional IDLs were introduced to manage the workload (not included in the product cost and quoting process). The per-piece cost of shipping raw material to the plant increased significantly. Small lots of material were brought in, and in many cases, material was purchased in volume to obtain price breaks; however, there were no firm orders to justify the purchases. The company was underquoting costs and, as a result, was winning a considerable amount of new business of this type. In the normal course of business, some customer orders were delayed and even canceled, but commissions and bonuses had already been paid. In short, the low-margin business did not generate sufficient margin money to cover the increased operating expenses. The sales force was receiving generous bonuses at the expense and detriment of the company. Other departments within the organization were not receiving bonuses because financial results were poor and goals were not met. In summary, revenue increased, margins declined, inventory rose, overhead expenses increased, and indirect labor grew to accommodate the new business generated.

The Fix—The bonus calculations were modified to compensate the sales force solely based on the margin money generated from new business. Commissions and bonuses were distributed only after customers paid for shipped products. Additionally, the percentage of potential payouts was reduced for high-mix, low-volume, low-material-cost products. In contrast, a higher bonus percentage was awarded for high-cost, high-margin new products. This adjustment helped focus the sales team toward securing business that was beneficial for the company and obtaining favorable customer payment terms. Furthermore, additional costs were included in the margin money calculation to improve expense coverage and accuracy across both the quoting process and bonus calculations. These changes arrested the problematic behavior.

Example 2—The operational team was given a goal with a bonus opportunity to increase productivity (shipping more product each day without increasing headcount). The bonus was paid monthly.

Results—More products began shipping almost immediately. The scrap percentage increased, inspection and material costs rose, and the purchasing and engineering departments' resources were consumed handling material dispositions and expediting. Worse yet, customer complaints increased due to quality issues with the shipped product. Despite these operational deteriorations, the operations team received bonuses.

The Fix—The efficiency measurement calculation was adjusted to include all products produced and scrapped. The costs for expediting materials, engineering, and purchasing were factored into the margin money calculations. To qualify for a bonus, the scrap rate and customer complaint percentages had to be equal to or below the baseline rates used in the goal calculations. This corrected the problematic behavior.

Be Measured in a Way That Can't Be Manipulated

For some reason, a certain percentage of people seek to manipulate the bonus calculation system to earn a bonus, rather than improving the targeted process. Bonuses should be self-funding, so care must be taken to use reports and calculations that cannot be manipulated to present false improvement results. Additionally, the measurement results should be audited for accuracy before a bonus payment is made. Let's take a look at an example.

Example—The purchasing department will receive a bonus for meeting the goal of reducing the cost of purchased raw materials by a specified percentage.

Results—The decision was made to estimate a year's worth of material needs and purchase all that material at once to secure a volume discount at a lower cost. The material was scheduled to arrive each month. The problem was that there were no annual customer contracts to cover the amount of material purchased. When the material arrived, the actual number of customer orders received was lower than the forecasted and purchased amount. Inventory levels increased throughout the year. The purchasing department received bonuses for the reductions in raw material costs achieved during the year. The goal was met. However, the problem was that the increased inventory was not utilized and was eventually classified as "excess and obsolete material," resulting in financial accruals to cover the increased inventory cost. The accruals had to be made at current material cost rates, which had increased. As a result, bonuses were paid, but the financial impact was significantly negative due to the accruals generated to cover the "excess and obsolete material." The company would have been better off paying the normal, higher price for raw materials and ordering them only when customer orders were received.

The Fix—Include the material inventory quantity and costs in the bonus calculation, and establish some guardrails around the goals; decrease the raw material purchase price without increasing inventory, and so on. Consider taking an additional step by establishing a transformation team with adequate representation to cover the full scope of purchasing, new supplier development, and certification processes. Clarify the goal's scope to provide guidance, such as reducing raw material costs for components that account for the top 20 percent of the product's total material costs. Additionally, collaborate with engineering to modify material specifications and supplier selection, thereby reducing material costs through design changes.

Make the goals and desired process changes tangible through innovation, teamwork, and a diverse range of disciplines working together toward a shared objective. In this case, the goal must be broader than just a purchasing goal to ensure success. Expand the goal to be more inclusive of the entire purchasing system, including those working in the subsystems, and ensure they share the same goal and bonus potential. Additionally, establish a regular cadence with the team to review progress toward the goal and ensure alignment on the team's direction.

Have a Time Frame That Matches the Goal

The goal time period should align with the bonus calculation period and the bonus payout. If these periods vary in length, the bonus program may not be optimal, leading to dissatisfaction for either the company or the employee and undermining the program's perceived value. One example will illustrate this point. This example was briefly mentioned earlier.

Example—A salesperson receives a commission for orders they bring into the company. The commission is calculated as a percentage of the margin generated on each order.

Results—The salesperson received quarterly payments based on the margin generated on each order. Standard margins were used to calculate the earned bonus. Some orders had material lead-times that extended beyond the bonus payout period, so the salesperson was paid a bonus before the product was manufactured and shipped to the customer. The salesperson received the bonus before collecting payment from the customer for products shipped during the quarter. Additionally, the bonus was calculated based on standard costs rather than the actual costs incurred for a specific order.

Some materials were purchased at prices that differed from the standard due to smaller lot sizes or expedited shipping, which bypassed the standard lower-cost shipping process. In some instances, customers canceled or postponed their orders due to market declines. Some customers paid their invoices very late, while others took unapproved discounts on their paid invoices.

Considering all these factors, the salesperson had already received the bonus, but the funds had not yet been collected to cover it. In some instances, the funds were never collected, meaning that part of the bonus payout was never truly earned. The standard costs used to calculate margin money were also inaccurate, sometimes excessively high and at other times too low, depending on the specific circumstances.

The Fix—The bonus program was modified to calculate margin money based on the actual cost for each work order, and the bonus payout was determined solely by the actual cash collected during the quarter. With these changes, the salesforce became highly attuned to payment terms, unauthorized discounts taken, order lot sizes, and more. They began collaborating with customers on order timing, lot sizes, payment terms, shipping methods, and other aspects of the order placement and payment collection cycle to maximize margins on each order.

Paid Promptly After Results Are Verified

This point is straightforward: When the agreed-upon goal and timeline are met, verify the results and distribute the bonus. If the bonus goal is to reach a specific profit level for the year, pay the bonus during the first week of the second month after the fiscal year ends or sooner. Once the year-end financial results are approved, distribute the bonus. If a bonus goal is to complete a project and meet established timelines and cost requirements, verify the results and pay the bonus promptly; do not wait until year-end to issue the bonus. Align completion timing with the bonus payout schedule. If a bonus goal is to meet specific improvement metrics each month, then pay out the bonus early in the following month after verifying the results.

Additional Comments

1. What happens if a monthly bonus for improved performance exceeds an agreed-upon baseline number, and then, when the bonus is paid out, the operation regresses, resulting in performance falling below the baseline the following month? Remember that a performance evaluation is intended to be an employer–employee agreement that details what happens when the goal is achieved and what happens when it is not. A company may decide not to pay bonuses for months in which performance goals are not met. In the spirit of following the concept, a bonus must be self-funded; a different company may design the bonus program to require that any lost margin money, caused by poor performance, be recovered before a future bonus can be paid. Both scenarios are acceptable, but the key is that the company and its employees should be aware of how different scenarios will be handled before the bonus program begins, if possible.
2. A manufacturing facility in Mexico was provided a bonus opportunity based on meeting its Earnings Before Interest, Taxes, Depreciation, and Accruals (EBITDA) goal for the year. The facility had spent over two years developing and introducing several proprietary new parts to the market and integrating them into customers' products. The products were well-received by customers, resulting in a surge in orders for the new products. The facility was finally set to receive an exceptional bonus, one that would be significantly above average, rewarding employees for their innovation and efforts in growing the company through the development of proprietary new products. Everyone was excited!

What happened was unexpected. The U.S. dollar (USD) weakened against the Mexican peso, which means expenses paid in pesos were now 20 percent to 25 percent higher when converted to USD for corporate financial roll-up reporting. The costs in Mexican pesos remained unchanged in the local financial reports. According to these reports, the facility overperformed its bonus goal and should have received a bonus payout exceeding 100 percent. However, the corporate financial reports indicated that the facility underperformed and did not meet the bonus payout threshold. If all economic figures had been calculated at the exchange rate used to set the bonus targets, the facility would have earned a favorable bonus. However, using the actual exchange rates experienced during the year, the results fell short of the goal.

How should one handle this situation? How does the company reward its employees for their innovation and efforts to attract new customers and introduce patented products to the marketplace, which will benefit the company for many years, especially when corporate financial reports indicate that financial goals were not met?

There is more to this story. The exchange rate for the upcoming year's budget was updated to the current exchange rate, which was favorable to the peso against the USD. For the next six months, all EBITDA measurements tracked to plan in both the Mexican and corporate financial reports, with the exchange rate remaining stable. However, during the last six months of the year, the USD regained strength and recovered its position against the peso. The expenses in Mexico remained unchanged in the Mexican financial statements, but in the corporate financial reports, the costs appeared favorable. At year-end, the corporate financial reports indicated that the Mexico operation ended the year very favorably, exceeding budget expectations and expected to earn over 100 percent of the bonus payout. However, the Mexican financial reports indicated otherwise; they did not meet the EBITDA goal on the Mexican financial books. The question now was how to be fair to both the company and the Mexican employees in this scenario.

The purpose of a bonus program is to reward individuals for achieving specific goals. Measuring that achievement requires careful attention to ensure accuracy and fairness. An improved approach might be to specify the exchange rate to be used throughout the entire evaluation period when setting goals, thereby maintaining consistency. This would normalize fluctuations in exchange rates over the year.

Finding solutions to these real issues, and others, is crucial to maintaining healthy bonus programs and ensuring the workforce feels valued and appreciated. Both employees and the company must perceive the bonus program as fair for it to succeed. The company's actual approach to the situations presented above will remain unwritten. This provides an opportunity for you, the reader, to consider how you would respond to these scenarios if you were the company executive, and then reflect on your feelings about that response if you were the employee.

Chapter Summary

- Properly applied bonus programs can be a tool used to help with transformation and improvement activities and to drive improved performance.
- Bonus programs should be managed using concepts from an employer–employee agreement.
- There are at least seven key points to a successful bonus program:
    - Be self-funded.
    - Include everyone who drives results.
    - Offer enough value to motivate.
    - Avoid rewarding bad behavior.
    - Be measured in a way that can't be manipulated.
    - Have a time frame that matches the goal.
    - Pay promptly after results are verified.
- Bonus programs must be viewed as fair and equitable by both the company and employees to be successful.

CHAPTER 12

Habits

My eight-year-old grandson came home from school one day and showed me a handful of stickers his teacher had given him. We sat down and reviewed the stickers together. One sticker in bright, colorful letters read, "Nothing changes if nothing changes." The more I thought about this, the more profound the quote became. And, so it is with our lives, companies, and everything else around us. For transformation and cultural change to occur, something must change.

All the effort that went into transforming the Salvarcar facility paid off. The facility survived and became a model of efficiency. After two to three years of work in the plant, attention shifted to the question of "What needs to occur to make all the transformations stick, with no backsliding?" In the normal course of business, managers and employees frequently change positions or companies. With their departure, there may be a tendency to backslide, either slightly or significantly. We did not want that to happen, so we implemented a business process that, if followed, would not only maintain the transformations and culture achieved but also drive continuous improvement: ongoing innovation and adaptation to technological advancements over time.

This brings us to the final key topic in this treatise on transformation and cultural change: the process that ensures these changes endure. The critical concept for ongoing success is developing good habits while eliminating mediocre and bad ones.

Achieving any significant goal requires designing a process of actions that leads to the goal, and then developing the habits to adhere to that process—nothing more, nothing less.

Many books have been written about habits, how they are formed, broken, and changed. There's no need to recap all that here. The primary goal is to establish habits within an organization that, when adhered to, will facilitate goal achievement, foster positive change, and effectively control processes. In short, the Engine of Transformation can be applied to develop and change habits in individuals and organizations alike. All things are the same, just the variables change.

As in the basketball free-throw example, mental imagery is a useful tool for conditioning the mind to form a habit. Mentally visualizing different scenarios that one might face and planning how to handle them helps maintain the desired habit response. This is a powerful technique. Consider one example as an illustration.

You have decided to reduce the quantity of sweets you eat. To help develop this habit, the home environment is modified to remove all sweets, ensuring a seamless maintenance of the new habit. The habit becomes more difficult to keep when at work or going out with friends. Work provides cakes for all employees' birthdays to celebrate their special days. Customers are welcome to enjoy pastries and soft drinks during their visits as part of a meet-and-greet social event. Visiting friends to play games usually includes bowls of sweets and chips to snack on.

Instead of deciding what to do in the moment, it is better to plan responses in advance for these situations. This way, you can rehearse your preferred responses, both mentally and physically, in advance. Participating in practice sessions will greatly increase the chances of responding positively when unexpected sweets appear. When a habit fails, take a moment to activate the EOT. Gather data, analyze what happened, and find out why the failure occurred. Innovate your process and controls to include the new expected responses. Keep the EOT moving forward, and over time, the habit will become nearly perfect in compliance.

The Salvarcar team identified the daily, weekly, and monthly meetings and actions required to review data, conduct training, walk the floor to meet with the workforce, analyze system and personnel performance, and more. The same set of actions was developed across all levels of the organization, from the shop-floor workforce to the site executive. After those were specified, they were incorporated into the business process control procedures to ensure that all actions and meetings became habitual and were performed as planned. Over time, as systems were analyzed and improved, the process specifications were modified and controlled accordingly. Through consistent use of the EOT, positive habits were developed in the daily tasks of individuals across the organization.

Our family has a friend who is a runner. This habit developed over the years, and she runs almost every day. One morning, while out on her regular run, the thought came to her mind, "Consistency is a mark of divinity." Over the years, I have reflected on that comment and concluded that being consistent in our actions and developing good habits and routines can elevate an individual and a company from good to better to the best we can be. We should all strive to be more divine.

Remember, "Nothing changes if nothing changes."

Chapter Summary

- It is following a process that leads to goal achievement.
- Specifications for daily actions can be developed for all in an organization.
- Developing habits is essential to controlling a process.
- Mental visualization techniques can help prevent habit failure.
- Process control principles can be used to establish and maintain habits.
- Nothing changes if nothing changes.

CHAPTER 13

Bringing It All Together

Our narration is coming to an end, but it's not over. Perhaps Yogi Berra said it better when he stated, "It ain't over till it's over." Implementing the information in this book worked well for the Salvarcar facility, helping it overcome its challenges and bad habits to become the best in its class. And it can work well for all who struggle to overcome their current limitations and improve. The struggle to improve is never finished; it continues daily.

We have touched on principles and tools for establishing a transformation system to enhance organizations and change culture. So, what's left to discuss? We didn't come all this way just to come all this way; let's bring it all together into one great, overarching plan. Then, it will be up to you, the reader, to apply the principles in this book and transform the systems you interact with and the culture around them.

Sequencing Implementation

The sequence of an implementation plan will change from situation to situation. The key is to look at where you are, then "lift where you stand." Just begin and move forward. Training and implementation plans can be modified as more is learned during the journey. This book was written in a generic implementation sequence that enables immediate implementation and movement. The sequence presented was:

- To make organizational transformation successful, the leader of the organization needs to understand that he or she is the leader of the effort and must be willing to participate in the process at all levels of the organization.
- A Transformation Council (TC) needs to be organized and led by the organization leader.

  - Communicate the tasks at hand using change management techniques.
  - Develop a vision and goals for the future of the organization's systems at all levels.
  - Teams should be officially organized, utilizing the nine parts of the team structure process, to develop plans and work on organizational transformation projects that align with the vision and goals.
  - Team leaders should report to the TC every two weeks on their progress toward their goal, any roadblocks they encounter, and express any needs they may have, receiving instructions accordingly.
- A transformation system requires carefully designed training subsystems for all levels of the organization that follow the successful model of Knowing, Seeing, and Feeling.
  - Knowing—receive written and verbal instruction on the proper method to use.
  - Seeing—see the proper method performed in detail.
  - Feeling—performing the proper method and receiving immediate feedback from an expert to help fine-tune the performance to the established method until it is done correctly.
- Audit measured performance and verify that the proper method is being followed.
- Develop training for a toolbox of techniques that can be used by teams throughout the entire organization.
- KPIs must be established and regularly monitored at all levels of the organization to ensure that processes remain under control.
- KPIs should be designed to control key processes; broad and inclusive, difficult to game, provide needed information, and in sufficient quantity to cover all aspects of the organization that need to be controlled, transformed, and improved.
- Resist the false tyranny of speed and find the correct speed of change that the organization is capable of functioning at. The speed of change will increase over time.
- No need to wait to begin transformation. Start where you are with what you have; then train and modify systems as you go.

- Following a process is what leads to goal achievement; focus on the process.
- Transforming a system or subsystem to an innovative, improved system involves key steps: Analyzing the current system state, dreaming of a future system state, innovating a process to bridge the gap between the two, and then controlling that process.
- Once the process to bridge to the innovative, improved system is designed and implemented, don't be afraid to modify it as required if new data indicates it should be.
- Where possible, use a training and progression matrix program to tie training, experience, skill, living company values, teamwork, and wages together in a way that permits employees to choose their career paths and speed of growth within the organization.
- Match pay levels to the criticality of the position to the organization.
- Move away from annual employee performance evaluations and toward a continuous employee performance appraisal system.
    - Choose three to four company values and make those an integral part of employee evaluations and the wage increase process.
    - Modify job descriptions to incorporate the company's values and describe what it means to embody each value in each job position. Include a JIM in job descriptions.
    - A JIM forms the core base for an employee evaluation program.
    - Develop employer–employee type documents for bonus programs that specify which KPI measurements, goals, or project completion objectives must be met and the corresponding percentage linked to each element included in the bonus.
    - Both the company and the employee should agree to and sign the bonus document. Ensure the responsibilities of both the employee and the company are clearly outlined in the document.
- Cultures are changed, and transformation gains are kept from backsliding by forming good habits and daily routines.
- Consistency is a mark of divinity. Develop consistency in following the established organizational processes to embody the

company values and execute all aspects of daily work. Good habits and good organizational processes lead to a bright future.
- Nothing is written in stone; transform systems and processes continually to take advantage of emerging technologies and innovative improvements at all levels.

What Now?

We have come to the conclusion of this book. But not to the conclusion of the transformation process. There are three parts to training and developing skills: Knowing, Seeing, and Feeling. This book addresses the first two by presenting information on the processes and tools used to transform organizational culture, and by sharing real-world experiences and results from their effective application.

What's left for you, the reader, is to Feel. Use this information to develop a transformation system. Use this book and other relevant resources as standards for comparison to provide expert feedback as you undergo your transformations.

Hopefully, this book will serve as a catalyst for continued learning on the topics presented. No recipe fits all situations. Create a system that works for your situation by breaking down an existing transformation system into lower-level subsystems, modifying each component, and reassembling the subsystems into a higher-level system tailored to your specific needs. Be innovative as you move forward.

The journey is never over. Once a goal is achieved, the EOT continues to move forward. An image of a new, innovative system appears on the horizon, and a new process is designed and controlled to realize it.

Enjoy the sights, sounds, and struggles of the never-ending journey. Remember, "We are the music makers, and we are the dreamers of dreams!"

Notes

1. Leslie Bricusse and Anthony Newley, "Pure Imagination," from *Willy Wonka and the Chocolate Factory,* 1971.
2. Arthur O'Shaughnessy, "Ode," 1873.
3. Gary Mack, *Mind Gym: An Athlete's Guide to Inner Excellence* (McGraw-Hill Books, 2001), 58.
4. Genrich Altshuller, *40 Principles TRIZ Keys to Technical Innovation*, TRIZ Tools, vol. 1 (Technical Innovation Center, Inc., 2002), 15–17.
5. Thomas A. Little, "10 Requirements for Effective Process Control," *Quality Progress*, February 2001.
6. L. Verdelle Clark, "Effect of Mental Practice on the Development of a Certain Motor Skill," *Research Quarterly. American Association for Health, Physical Education and Recreation*, 31, no. 4 (1960): 560–569.
7. John Wooden and Steve Jamison, *Wooden: A Lifetime of Observations and Reflections on and Off the Court* (McGraw-Hill Books, 1997), 199.
8. Seth Davis, *Wooden, A Coach's Life* (Times Books, 2014), 15.
9. Dieter F. Uchtdorf, "Lift Where You Stand," *General Conference of the Church of Jesus Christ of Latter-Day Saints*, November 2008, https://www.churchofjesuschrist.org/study/general-conference/2008/10/lift-where-you-stand?lang=eng.
10. W. Edwards Deming, *Out of the Crisis*, 2nd ed. (MIT Press, Kindle editions, 2000), 91, 87.
11. W. Edwards Deming, "The Merit System: The Annual Appraisal: Destroyer of People," in *The Essential Deming: Leadership Principles from the Father of Quality*, ed. Joyce Nillson Orsini. (McGraw-Hill, 2013), 27.
12. Peter R. Scholtes, W. Edwards Deming, and Malcolm S. Knowles, *The Team Handbook* (Joiner Associates, Inc., 1996), introduction.
13. Stephen Covey, "Beyond the Performance Review", *Chief Talent Officer*, August 1, 2005, https://www.chieftalentofficer.co/2005/08/01/beyond-the-performance-review/.

Index

www.ingramcontent.com/pod-product-compliance
Lightning Source LLC
LaVergne TN
LVHW012332100826
845148LV00017B/2117